FASHION
UNRAVELED

Jennifer Lynne Matthews

Publication by East Bay Fashion Resource
Oakland, California

How to Start, Run and Manage an Independent Fashion Label

Cover Design by Helen Munch-Ellingson

Book Design by Designarchy

Services for our readers:

Colleges, fashion schools, wholesale purchasing:
The East Bay Fashion Resource offers special rates
for universities, fashion schools and wholesale purchasing.

Updates:
Information contained in this book was current at the time
of publishing. For updates, check our website.

Contact us:
East Bay Fashion Resource
261 10th Street, Suite 302
Oakland, CA 94607
Phone: 510-834-8443
Fax: 510-280-7295
info@eastbayfashionresource.com

Publication by East Bay Fashion Resource

ISBN-10: 0615273106

ISBN-13: 978-0-615-27310-5

Library of Congress Control Number: 2009900314

Acknowledgments

Special thanks to everyone who has supported me through my business and this book.

Misty Rose, I couldn't have gotten past the outline without your help.

Helen Munch-Ellingson, I couldn't have had such a killer cover design without you, or such killer times in the Mission.

Tania Kac, my talented book designer, your patience with me is blessed.

Ashley Burke, your timing isn't the best, but I always love to hear from you. You are my favorite sister.

Greg Matthews, my favorite accountant and father, your belief in me pushed me to become the woman I am.

Kathy Matthews, your support and our pedicures saved my life.

Kirtley Wienbroer, you were there when I needed someone most. Thanks so much for being a part of my life.

Blakely Bass and Tessa Poppe, for being my closest friends. We will always entertain each other.

Irene Hernandez-Feiks, you have been my biggest supporter and kept encouraging me when I was at my wits' end. Thanks for that.

Thanks to all my contributors: M Herrera, Amy Cools, Susan Schwartz, Jenny Hwa, Julie Busch, Shveta Shourie, Elizabeth Sullivan, Lorraine Sanders, Hazel Grace Dircksen and Robert Ruggani.

And to all those who helped, encouraged and assisted in getting me to publish this book: Michelle Bond, Allie Covarubbius, Yetunde Schuhmann and last but not least, my students at FIDM who are my inspiration.

Contents

How to Use This Book

I have organized this book, not in the exact order of developing a business plan, but in the order of organizing your thoughts to start a fashion business. I start by helping you determine who you are, your strengths, and the qualities that define you as a person equipped to run a business. You will develop your business plan by looking at these strengths and qualities.

Together, we will review each section in detail. I provide forms in several sections of the book to assist you in this process. I have also made the forms available on our website for your convenience (www.eastbayfashionresource.com). Fill out each of these forms as thoroughly as possible before proceeding to the next chapter. If you must stop and conduct additional research, please take the time to do so. Your research will help you through the process of building your business concept.

In the margins of this book, I have provided links to websites and informational articles. I have also provided experts' opinions, as well as real world examples to help you understand this business more thoroughly. Because I have experienced the process of getting a fashion business off the ground first hand, I feel confident that my experiences will make your endeavors less daunting.

Throughout this book I offer advice based on my personal experience. It is not to be construed as legal advice by any means. It is best to consult a lawyer for any legal issues concerning your business.

My Story

My story starts in 1999. I attended New York City's Fashion Institute of Technology, studied fashion design and graduated in 1999. After a very brief stint working for a designer, preceded by a very lengthy process of finding that job, I decided I was not meant to work for anyone but myself.

Fast forward three years. I had moved to San Francisco and decided it was time to start my own fashion design business. I read every book out there on the subject, met with advisors and consultants, hired a patternmaker to review my patterns, and answered every single ad on Craigslist.com for designers.

Where did this get me? $20,000 in the hole, following a series of financial mistakes due to advisors telling me I was ready to launch my business. I had invested in that beautiful silk fabric and that French lace I wanted so badly, only to discover that my customer was so off target, I didn't sell a single thing. No book told me, nor did any consultant warn me of the complexities of what I was getting ready to dive into.

One year later, I had to step away from my business and reevaluate what I was doing. Unfortunately, I had already made the financial mistake previously mentioned. I regrouped, started a restaurant job, and put every extra cent I had into my business.

The damage wasn't over yet. A few years went by, I had my designs in several stores, and then an opportunity crossed my path. Without any planning, I decided over the course of a Christmas party to open up my very own boutique. What better place to showcase my designs than my own storefront, right? WRONG.

Two years later, I closed my doors. The store had evolved into a really cool designer cooperative boutique where a dozen designers took turns working and sharing store responsibilities. But I was doing nothing for my clothing line, my sanity, or my bank account. I had maxed out my credit cards just to keep the doors open. Once I closed the store, I was able to see that opening it in the first place was something that I should never have done.

I am now an educator, a mentor, a designer and a successful business woman. My goal is to help you avoid the mistakes I made.

—Jennifer Lynne
Designer & Owner, Porcelynne Lingerie, www.porcelynne.com
Business Consultant, East Bay Fashion Resource,
www.eastbayfashionresource.com

INTRODUCTION TO THE FASHION INDUSTRY

Chapter 1
Background and Statistics

Fashion design is a relatively new profession in the eyes of the government. Up until the 1980s the professions that were recognized were tailors and dressmakers. Even in the 1980s and 1990s, the government grouped all forms of designers in to one tax category. This included interior, graphic, and fashion designers.[1]

The first fashion design program was started in 1904 at Parsons School of Design in New York. It was founded as a creative and artistic extension to the industrial revolution. The number of schools that now offer fashion design programs in the United States are well over 100, with new fashion programs added every year.

The more recent attention to this industry was brought forth by the *Bravo* TV series *Project Runway* which began airing in 2004. (Here's a fun tidbit – yours truly made it through round one of auditions and received a call-back for Season 6 on their new network, *Lifetime*). Art and design schools today are seeing an increase in enrollment in the major of fashion design, as well as an increase in graduates. Many of these graduates aspire to start their own businesses after graduation. Unfortunately, many of the schools churning out designers have yet to adopt an entrepreneurship program to help ensure their graduates' success in running their own businesses.

The most common misconception about the fashion industry is that is it glamorous and it will make you famous. If you are expecting either of these, you will be in for a surprise. Fashion designers seldom become famous and commonly work long hours, often just to make ends meet.

Many designers who get into the fashion industry, with the intent to start their own business, have not thought this through. Many don't know how to plan for the future, and very few know anything about running a business. This lack of planning and education is the reason 95% of design businesses fail. This is an alarming statistic, but there's a good reason behind it. Fashion design is not a business you just start overnight.

Here's a reality check. You are about to become a business owner. You will be spending more than 90% of your time running your business and less than 10% of your time designing (and in many cases that percentage is closer to 1% or 2%). After reading this book, hopefully, that 90% will look just a little bit easier.

Footnote
1   Statistical data obtained from the U.S. Bureau of the Census (Statistical Abstract: 91st Edition (1970), 110th Edition (1990), 120th Edition (2000)

Chapter 2
Summary of the Design Process

In this age of instant gratification and everything at your fingertips, it is common to forget that the process of creating a product—in the fashion industry or any other—takes much longer than just a click of a button. On average, an independent designer takes one to two years to go from the initial design concept to a completed product ready for sales.

The first step in creating a design collection is to research the current trends and make an educated prediction of what the trends will evolve into. Trend reporting services are available, but are often costly for independent designers to acquire. These reports "predict" what the popular styles, colors, and fabrics will be for a particular season, many times reporting up to 10 years in advance. (I explain trends and trending services more thoroughly in Chapter 7, Develop a Collection.)

The second step is sourcing, or finding resources for the fabrics and trims in your collection. The development of the collection has begun. Whether you develop patterns and samples on

Notes:

Notes:

your own, or work with an independent technical designer; you must create prototypes for the entire collection and test them for fit and design. The samples usually go through several changes before the final products are chosen. Many designs are changed and sometimes even canceled before they hit the production room floor. (This is covered in detail in the section on production, starting at Chapter 12.)

These samples are then marketed to retail buyers. They can be marketed at trade shows, through showrooms, through independent reps, or directly to a store. Retailers place their orders up to six months prior to the actual season when they plan to sell the collection. These orders specify the quantity of the product you will produce and when the retailer expects delivery.

Throughout these steps, fashion designers may have varying levels of involvement from design to production. The involvement depends on the size of the design company and the designer's experience. Designers working in small firms, or those new to the job, usually perform most of the technical, patternmaking, and sewing tasks themselves, in addition to designing the clothing. The larger the company, the more the work is distributed.

Even if a designer does not do the technical work, he or she still needs the knowledge of the entire process to exercise quality control and to ensure the desired outcome for the finished product.

DEVELOPING YOUR LINE

Chapter 3
Define Yourself

Before you even start thinking about how you will get your product out into the world, you need to figure out what your strengths are as a designer, a salesperson, a manager, and as a business owner. When defining your strengths, you should also be aware of your weaknesses.

Take time to really pinpoint what you know a lot about, what you know little about, and what you don't know at all. Even though you may not be strong in all areas, it doesn't mean you don't have what it takes to start your business. Learning how to delegate and contract out work is crucial. As smart and determined as you are, you cannot do everything yourself. Know up front what you need help with so you can focus on the things you know and enjoy best.

So how do you know when to delegate and share responsibilities? The decision will vary depending on your specific circumstances. Everyone's experience with delegating work is different. I didn't learn how to do so until almost my third year in business, but I can assure you I wished I had done it sooner.

Notes:

In the following example, M explains that trust was his biggest challenge in learning to share the load.

Real World Example

Designer: Michael Herrera, "M"

Company: M the Movement, www.mthemovement.com

The biggest challenge in running my own business was learning how to trust others enough to delegate. I am, like most artists, very critical of my work. It is very difficult for me to forgive myself, let alone other artists on my team, when my art /design is compromised. I have to dot every "i" and cross every "t", and in my eyes everything can always be improved. Even when you seem to be satisfied with an outcome, you see it in a completely different light the next day. Art is ever changing and this makes it that much harder to delegate because your team has to have the same "eye", tenacity, and dedication as you, and this is often hard to find.

I was able to "get over" this hump simply by life taking over. There will always come a point in your company's growth when you can't physically be everywhere at once, and so I had no choice but to let others take over certain projects. Little by little, I became better at "letting go." My company became a more efficient one. My life became more relaxed too. You need a start with a good team that understands your vision and supports it. With a team behind you, you can do anything.

M has worked in the fashion industry for 15 years and has designed for many design houses including Karl Kano, Michael Schumacher for Ferrari and Puma. In 2006, M turned his own design concepts into his own business. In two short years, M's business has established a celebrity clientele and a continuous stream of press coverage.

Define yourself

In defining who you are, be aware of both your strengths and your weaknesses. Check off whether each item is a strength or a weakness. Explain in detail why you chose as you did.

Design through illustration/art
- ☐ Strength
- ☐ Weakness

Explain: --

Design through flat pattern and/or draping
- ☐ Strength
- ☐ Weakness

Explain: --

Selling
- ☐ Strength
- ☐ Weakness

Explain: --

Researching
- ☐ Strength
- ☐ Weakness

Explain: --

Financial Planning/Managing
- ☐ Strength
- ☐ Weakness

Explain: --

Marketing
- ☐ Strength
- ☐ Weakness

Explain: --

Other
- ☐ Strength
- ☐ Weakness

Explain: --

Chapter 4
Define Your Market

What does "defining your market" mean? Determining the <u>price point</u> at which your product will sell and where it will sell is considered your market.

You probably have an idea of where you want to sell your product, but there are several factors which determine whether you can actually place your product into that market. Your fabric choices, construction details, and quality of production are the major factors in determining your design market.

Design Market

The design market can be broken down into several sub-markets. Below are brief definitions of some of the design markets; which price point they fit, and which retail outlets they can be found in.

Couture describes fine tailoring and custom made-to-order garments. Fabrics are of exquisite nature and may include hand-made laces. These garments are not found in department stores, but in <u>ateliers</u>. Most details are finished by hand, and not by machine. Today this term is being so loosely used, that it has lost its meaning and people have forgotten its true definition.

Price Point: The price range which determines the various markets from low end to high end, including budget, moderate, bridge, or designer.

Atelier: A Parisian studio and workroom

Did you know?

The term *haute couture* is protected by French law and is defined by the *Chambre de Commerce et d'Industrie de Paris*. The criterion for being labeled haute couture was established in 1945.

To earn the right to call oneself a couture house and to use the term *haute couture*, one must be invited to be a member of the *Chambre* and is required to follow each of these guidelines:

- Design made-to-order items for private clients, with one or more fittings.

- Have an *atelier* (studio) in Paris that employs at least fifteen people full-time.

- Present a collection to the Paris press twice a year; comprising at least thirty-five designs for both daytime and evening wear.

Presently, there are less than a dozen members by this definition.

Ready to Wear describes any garments that are manufactured in quantity. Ready to wear (RTW) can be split into several sub-categories:

Designer describes well known brands such as Gucci, Chanel and Louis Vuitton. Their price point is high and can range into the thousands for one garment. Customers are often wealthy and have disposable income. Fabrics are of a high quality and are costly. These designer brands can be found in high end boutiques or brand-name department stores such as Barneys, Saks, and Nordstrom's.

Bridge or *Contemporary* describes a market catering to a larger customer base. Price points are lower than designer and can range in the hundreds for one piece. The fabrics are of high quality. Many brands launched by celebrities such as Paris Hilton and Ed Hardy are considered to be contemporary. These design brands can be found in department stores such as Neiman Marcus, Bergdorf Goodman, and specialty boutiques.

Moderate describes a wide customer base and comprises much of the clothing market. Many independent designers fall in the moderate design market, along with Tommy Hilfiger and Jones of New York. The price points are moderate and fabrics are of medium quality. Designs of this sort can be found in shopping malls and smaller independent boutiques.

Budget describes an inexpensive market which can be found at large chain stores such as Forever 21 and H&M. Budget designs are also sold at mall chains such as Abercrombie & Fitch. Price points are usually under $100 per garment. Fabrics are cheap, and garments are generally poorly made. These garments are sometimes referred to as disposable clothing.

Mass Market describes off-price clothing, <u>seconds</u>, and closeouts. These designs can be found at stores such as Marshalls, TJ Maxx, and Ross. Merchandise is sometimes flawed or last season and is priced to move quickly. The price range is generally around or under $20 per piece.

Private Label brands are manufactured designs commissioned by stores who want to sell under their own brand name. The price points and actual markets can vary vastly. This has become a popular option for independent designers because they often have smaller collections and can offer exclusive designs to

Notes:

Seconds: *damaged goods, returns, last season's leftovers*

Notes:

Notes:

----

a store or boutique. Many department stores carry private label designs.

Each of these markets is further broken down into separate classifications. Here is a short list to help you decide where to introduce your collection. Please note that this is an abridged list and it can vary from market to market.

Womens: Juniors, Misses, Petites, Plus Size, Casuals, Tees, Suits, Maternity, Intimate Apparel, Activewear, Outerwear, Eveningwear

Mens: Big & Tall, Outerwear, Casuals, Tees, Suits

Children: Infant, Toddler, Girls, Boys, Toys

Accessories: Bags, Shoes, Hats, Scarves, Gloves

Define your market

Answer these questions to the best of your knowledge.

1. Do you see your product selling in a particular geographical area (locally, nationally, internationally, or a specific city)?

----

2. What sales outlets do you see your product selling well in (i.e. department stores, boutiques, online, etc.)?

----

3. What specific stores do you see your product selling in?

----

4. What design market do the above three answers place you in and why?

❑ Couture ❑ Designer ❑ Contemporary ❑ Moderate ❑ Budget ❑ Private Label

----

----

5. What area in this design market are you targeting? Be specific (e.g. juniors, plus size, etc.)

❑ Women --
❑ Men --
❑ Children --
❑ Accessories --

6. What types of items do you plan to create (pants, dresses, etc.)?

Chapter 5
Define Your Customer

The first question you should ask yourself is: Who is your customer? If your answer is "everyone," you have not done enough research. Hopefully, by the end of this chapter, you will begin to develop a better idea of who that person is.

Understanding your customer is just as important as developing your product. If you can not define a customer, you can not focus your marketing, create your patterns and fit, develop your color palette, or figure out where to sell your merchandise.

Your customer may change during the progress of your development, but that is to be expected. At this stage in the process, you are most likely unaware of what it will cost to produce your collection and therefore uncertain of the price point it will fall in. This alone is the primary reason why your customer might change. Keep an open mind throughout this process as nothing is set in stone and everything is meant to evolve.

While defining your customer, look through magazines—fashion, lifestyle, home magazines, or anything that you may have lying

Notes:

around. Pull out images that describe your customer's life and make a collage out of them. This type of collage is a visual way of telling others who your customer is. It will help you – as well as your graphic designer—when you begin the branding and marketing process.

Now that you have your images, use them as a reference to fill out the customer profile form at the end of this chapter. You may wish to use a pencil. There is a 99% probability that you will revise these answers by the time you finish with this book, so don't write in ink, unless it's one of those really cool Erasermates.

One thought that might occur to you is, "I want several different types of people to wear my clothes, not just one specific person!" Not every customer you get will fit into the description of your target customer, but they may *want* to be that kind of person. In my own business, I have defined my target customer as a working woman between the ages of 25 and 40 who earns around $45,000 per year. My customers, however, range from 16 to 60 years old and have consisted of students as well as women earning over $200,000 annually.

Not knowing who your customer is could set you up for a financial mistake. In the following example, Amy's vision of her customer created the largest obstacle for her business, before she got it right.

Real World Example

Designer: Amy Cools

Company: AC Clothing and Bags, www.acclothingandbags.com

The biggest challenge I encountered when I launched my business was learning to be flexible in my vision of my customer. Not so much of the artistic aspect of my design, but who and where my customers were. I theorized about where my customers shopped and what they wanted before observing and testing the market. I wanted a store before I was ready, and I rushed into it thinking my vision alone would make my venture a success.

As time passed and I gained experience, I learned that it is not only possible, but crucial to be flexible and to react to opportunities. When I started selling online, I discovered—to my surprise—that some of my most eager customers were in places I never considered my target areas. I also discovered that I enjoy traveling with my line and selling at events much more than selling at a single brick-and-mortar store. I closed my store to focus my energy on the customers I discovered through online sales. To sum up, my unexpected customers taught me the most about what it takes to be a fulfilled and successful designer – listening, and being flexible.

Amy is a self-taught designer that has been working independently in fashion for over 10 years. Amy's collections mix contemporary and vintage fabrics and are of a playful and colorful nature.

Customer Profile

Create your ideal customer. This will not limit who your customer is, but will help your focus.

Name: ....

Age: ....

Sex: ☐ Female ☐ Male

Marital Status: ☐ Single ☐ Married ☐ Separated ☐ Divorced ☐ Widowed

Occupation: ....

Annual Income: ....

Geographic Location: ....

Buying Habits:

Lifestyle:

Leisure Activities:

Vacation Destinations:

Favorite Designers:

Favorite Stores:

Chapter 6
Create Your Brand and Identity

What is a brand and how do you create one? In a nutshell, a brand is anything and everything that separates your business from the rest. Your brand creates an identity and explains who you are, what you do and why you do it. You may believe a brand is just a logo, but it is so much more.

Creating an identity is every bit as important as creating your product. Approaching your business with a branding strategy before you start your product development can be a wise choice. Keeping consistent values in your business and always representing your business in the same manner creates recognition and loyalty.

Think of your business as you would think of a celebrity, let's say Angelina Jolie. We associate her with good causes. Beware of making bad moves. People will often remember you by the mistakes you make and overlook the positives (Britney Spears – mouseketeer gone bad). Avoid this by carefully hammering out your company values, your message, your product, your website, and everything else in between.

Based on an interview with Susan Schwartz, Branding expert, You Who Branding, YouWhoBranding.com

Notes:

Notes:

Once you have developed your company values, proceed directly to go, collect $200, then begin to develop your name and logo. Your own name should be first on your list, but you can also choose a word or phrase that is representative of you and/or your product. Choose a variety of names that you like and pre-screen them with family and friends. Before deciding on your name, do internet searches and make sure you aren't using a competitor's name.

Fictitious Business Name:
A name under which you operate your business that is not the same as your given name. It is commonly referred to as a DBA (doing business as).

You can search the fictitious business name database for your district (city, county or state) to make sure another company registered in your area is not using the same name. I will explain how to register a fictitious business name in Chapter 30.

Hot Tip!

Once you settle on a name, buy a domain name (name for your website) ASAP. You don't want to lose it to someone with the same idea. Focus on a .com, and as a last resort; use a .net or another ending.

Notes:

Your next step is to design a logo representative of your chosen name. A logo is a unique and characteristic font and/or image in which your name should always be rendered. If you have a background in graphic design, you can try to tackle this, but otherwise, leave it up to an expert. What you think may look fabulous may not appear that way to a buyer or to the media. You want to convey a level of status and professionalism in your logo design. To do this properly, you may need to invest a few hundred dollars in an experienced graphic designer. It will be money well spent. Your logo will be your face to the world—do it professionally.

I also mentioned an image. The image is a symbol that represents your logo and name. This is usually part of the logo, but can be used as a stand-alone on your clothing labels, business cards, or your website to represent your name if the full logo isn't suitable for the placement. This isn't always needed, but it's recommended, especially if the name is not short. Branding images you may be familiar with are Nike's swoosh logo, Levi's pocket red tab, and Joe Boxer's smiley face.

Last but not least is your choice of color. Consider colors that speak to the nature of your business. If you are not sure what these might be, start by researching the meanings of certain colors and the type of emotions they generate. This is called color psychology. (Actually, much of this industry can directly be linked to psychology, but I'll save that topic for another book.)

Here is a brief outline describing colors and their meanings.

Red – This color is bold and draws attention. It shows off your confidence and passion.

Orange – Orange is a color of unity and harmony.

Yellow – Brighter yellow symbolizes cheer. Mellow yellows convey stability.

Green - Represents growth, development, and motivation.

Blue – Blue is associated with introspection and tranquility.

Purple –This color is associated with creativity and spirituality.

Pink – Pink is soothing and nurturing.

Gray – Gray invokes balance and safety.

Brown –This color represents grounding and security.

Black – Black exudes mystery, authority, depth, and strength.

White – White is the color of trust.

Notes:

Read more about Color Psychology at http://www.infoplease. com/spot/colors1.html

Notes:

Branding

What company names are you considering?

What is your company's story? How did it evolve?

What is your vision for your company?

What are your company's values and what do you promise with your product?

What kind of customer will identify with your brand?

What makes your company and product stand out?

What is the purpose of your product?

Chapter 7
Develop a Collection

You've defined yourself, your brand, your market and your customer. It's time to develop your collection.

Launching a product line with too many items is the downfall of many designers. Setting limits of 3-5 silhouettes in 2-4 fabrics is a good place to start. Remember that even in these 8-12 pieces you will need to produce a full size range. This can easily add up to over 30 pieces, so you can see why you might want to limit your first collection.

Silhouette: *The shape of the garment*

Have you thought about what triggers your creativity and what inspires you as a designer? Are you inspired by fabrics or colors? Is it your tactile or your visual sense that guides you? Regardless of where you pull your inspiration from, there comes a moment in every designer's process when you hit a creative wall. Try creating "Inspiration Books." These books can be compiled of fashion images, vacation spots, photography layouts, or anything else that inspires you.

Notes:

In your collection development, don't limit yourself in your designing. Expect to create five times the number of designs that you will actually take to production. You will gradually

Notes:

cut designs from your collection, but this is to be expected. Narrowing down your collection is part of the design process and can be done in several different and creative ways.

Try conducting small focus groups with friends or your target customers. Hiring a firm to conduct a focus group is swell, but highly expensive. An alternative is to use Craigslist.org to find your target customers. Post an ad pinpointing a specific customer and offer incentives for participation in your focus group. Free merchandise or gift cards are some ways you can lure participants. If you have developed an email marketing list and have an online store, you could offer discounts to customers who fill out an online survey, which you can create using companies like www.SurveyMonkey.com.

Many larger businesses use trending services to help with their collection development. These trending services predict which colors will be used several seasons down the road. They also dictate popular silhouettes for the season as well as the textiles that will be used. Have you ever noticed that items you purchase on sale from last season never match anything? Color schemes are developed through the trending services and all colors in one season are meant to be interchanged with each other, regardless of the designer. Items from season to season are not meant to match.

Fashion, Fabric, and Trend Reporting Services:
http://www.fabricstockexchange.com/index.php?page=links_details&ID=4

There are trend forecasting books available for around the thousand dollar mark. Another possibility is to consult with services such as Peclers, Promostyl, Trend Union or WGSN.

Many independent designers choose not to follow these trend reporting services however, for several reasons other than being outrageously expensive. One, we consider ourselves unique, do not wish to follow trends, and want our products to stand out. Two, we purchase our fabrics from what is available, from textile companies that have already followed the trending services. Three, we are closer to the manufacturing process than the larger companies, so we can react to trends already on the market and cater to them as opposed to planning out our collections years in advance.

Notes:

Food for Thought:

Can you imagine predicting what will be the best selling item for 2019? It seems a bit of a stretch to think that far, but fashion trends are often planned and are not by accident. Which makes you wonder why these "fortune tellers" keep bringing back fashion faux pas from the past like dropped crotch pants, the dress that makes everyone look pregnant, and silly things like jelly shoes and scrunchies!

Chapter 8
Development Schedule

There are four main seasons in fashion: fall, holiday, spring, and summer. You may sometimes see additional "seasons" such as resort, pre-spring, or pre-fall. These are usually set up for in between deliveries. When you are first starting out, don't try to design for all four seasons—you will drive yourself mad as well as go broke in the process. Focus on one collection in your first year of business. This collection will most likely be your test as to whether you have nailed your market and customer. There is no sense in wasting your hard earned money on more than one collection if there is the slight chance you could be targeting the wrong market.

In Between Deliveries: The time in between major seasons during which retailers wish to receive shipments of goods.

Planning your collection is done far in advance, sometimes up to a year. There are markets or tradeshows that coincide with each of the major seasons. These markets are held 4-6 months prior to the season of release or delivery. Jewelry and accessory markets are held closer to the delivery date, usually 4-6 weeks. Below is a chart that gives a typical schedule as it applies to collection planning. At the end of this section, I have

Delivery: The window of time that retailers accept shipments for the upcoming season.

Development Calendar for the Standard Garment Industry

This table represents 4 seasons in production. During each stage of a collection, design firms are working on a second, or even third collection simultaneously.

Months:	Jan	Feb	Mar	Apr	May	Jun	Jul	Aug	Sep	Oct	Nov	Dec
Designing	▓	▓		░	░		■	■				
Patterns & Samples		▓	▓		░		■	■				
Sales	■	■							■	■		
Production		▓	▓		░	░						
Ship	■	■	■									

provided an estimated timeline for the development of an independent designer collection.

More recently, mainly due to the economy, small retail buyers at trade shows aren't ordering as much far in advance and are opting for immediates. This is both good and bad for the industry. It's good for smaller independent designers because we have a much closer handle on our production and can usually handle a quicker turnaround time for production. It's bad for the large fashion houses because they don't have access to these turnarounds. Many of the larger companies produce overseas, so production is not as hands-on.

Immediates imply that the designer has already gone into production before orders have been placed. This can be risky. What if your product is completely off kilter and you've ended up investing your entire budget into a collection that doesn't sell? On the other hand, if you nailed your market and customer, you could be seeing a positive cash flow even sooner than expected.

Immediates:
Merchandise that is available within 4-6 weeks

Turnaround Time:
Length of time from the beginning of the production cycle until products are available for delivery

Notes:

Independent Designer Production Schedule

This represents one full production cycle in a 12 month period, a second production cycle begins when production starts for the first collection. Depending on a designer's start date, the months may vary so they have been represented as numbers instead of months.

Months:	1	2	3	4	5	6	7	8	9	10	11	12
Designing	██	██					██	██				
Patterns & Samples	██	██					██					
Sales			██	██	██				██	██	██	
Production						██	██	██				██
Ship									██	██		
Direct Sales									██	██	██	██

Chapter 9
Competition

You've researched your customer and your market; now let's talk about your competition. To put the most important question bluntly, who would you like to take customers away from? Use the worksheet at the end of this section to evaluate your closest competition. These should be companies that you see selling in the same market you have targeted and at a similar price point.

Think about this: Is there room for your product in this market? Is your product different from what's already out there? What's your niche? Write a list of things that make you stand out. Is it your business practices? Your fabric choices? The fit of your garments?

Educate yourself on what's available in your market. Walk your local shopping district. Ask the retailers which items are their best and worst sellers and why they think that is. Could it be the colors? The price? The quality? Asking these questions will save you money and time in the long run. In other words: Do your &#$@&^$% research! You'll thank yourself later, I guarantee it.

Notes:

Competition

Competition:

    Strenghts:

    Weaknesses:

Competition:

    Strenghts:

    Weaknesses:

Competition:

    Strenghts:

    Weaknesses:

Competition:

    Strenghts:

    Weaknesses:

PRODUCTION

Chapter 10
Introduction to Production

It's time to rub the magic lamp and ask the genie to make your products. In the magical world of Aladdin, our garments are made an in instant. Since most of us live in the concrete world of Earth, we have to take the traditional route and create our garments through a production process.

To begin production, you must find sources for your fabrics and notions, develop patterns for your collection and create samples. In the following chapters, I will cover each of these steps in detail and help guide you through the production process.

Notes:

Chapter 11
Fabric Sourcing

Sourcing can be a scary subject especially if you don't have access to a garment district and are limited to high priced chain fabric stores. Let's be honest, if you live in LA or NYC, you shouldn't have a problem, but if you live in Middle America, where do you find your sources? Don't fret, there are several options for you yet.

Option 1: Find it at a tradeshow Textile shows are the ideal way to source your fabrics. At a show, such as the Los Angeles International Textile Show, you get a chance to see everything in one place. It can be a bit overwhelming, so having an idea of what you are looking for in the first place is a must. Here are some questions to consider:

What colors are you leaning towards?
Are you seeking woven fabrics or knit fabrics?
What quality of fabric are you looking for? Is it fine silks, organic fabrics, or run-of-the-mill broadcloths?

A visit to your local stores should help you narrow your decisions. Don't stop at just one—hit them all. At many places, you can ask for a swatch of the fabric. Make a note of the width

Sourcing: trade jargon for finding resources for your fabric, notions, and everything in between.

Infomat.com— online resources for trade shows and industry research

Notes:

of fabric, the fiber content, where you bought it, the price, and any notes on availability. You may need to buy yardage at a moment's notice for a last minute order and it's a good idea to know whether, and where, you can get the fabric quickly.

At the end of this chapter I've added a textile sourcing form to help you organize this information.

After you've done a local run and narrowed down your choices, plan a trip to the nearest textile show. These shows carry everything from notions and cheap polyester to high quality laces, "green" fabrics, and everything in between. If you aren't prepared, you could get lost in the chaos.

Option 2: Find a jobber What, might you ask, is a "jobber"? A jobber is a wholesale distributor who buys fabric lots from leftover productions or last season fabric. This can be a great choice for you if you are doing smaller quantities. One question you may ask is, "Can I reorder this fabric?" The most common answer is, no. These fabrics are seconds, what you see is what you get.

At times, a jobber might offer to track down a fabric for you, but it will often be at retail prices. So if you see it, buy it, and buy all of it. On occasion, once you develop a relationship with a jobber, he or she may offer to buy fabric back from you or trade it out, but usually at pennies of what you paid.

Some fabric stores may act as jobbers. Many smaller mom and pop shops may offer their merchandise for purchase at wholesale prices or at a discount.

Option 3: Find a fabric rep A fabric rep will usually represent several different textile companies and travel on the road to secure new clients. If you attend a textile show, the show guide should list the fabric reps who exhibited there, but how do you find them if you are miles away from everything? Strangely enough, fabric reps are generally listed in the yellow pages, so you can locate one near you. You can also search online for companies that carry the textiles you want. Contact them to see if they have a fabric rep that covers your area. If they do, you are in luck. If they don't, you might consider becoming a rep for them. If you can't find someone to do what you need, why not do it yourself and make a little cash on the side? You would then be listed on their website and people will find you.

Option 4: Find it online If you are at your wits' end and cannot make it to a fabric show, and can't find a jobber or a fabric rep to help you, give it a go with internet searches. Ebay.com and Etsy.com can sometimes have just the fabric you need, but there are many other resources available, so do some googling.

Now that you have found the sources for your fabric, you need to know what questions to ask. This pertains to fabric show reps and jobbers, too.

What are their minimums? Many companies you find at fabric shows require a ridiculous minimum yardage, some in the quantities of 1000 yards or more. You can sometimes get around this by ordering sample yardage. Sample yardages can be as low as one yard or as much as 100. Sample cuts are usually more expensive, or they may charge you a fee to cut the smaller yardage. Either way, expect to pay more.
A second way to get around ordering minimum fabric in each color is to order the fabric as PFD (prepared for dying). PFD refers to the fabric's dye-ability. If you plan on offering several designs in the same fabric but in different colors, you can have

Notes:

End Lot: The last of the fabric by a supplier. It is the last of it that has been produced, and will not be made again.

Relaxing Fabric: Knits are wound tight and will sometimes shrink when unrolled. Letting them sit unrolled for 48 hours brings the fabric to its natural state.

your garments dyed after being sewn. Buying PFD will often help you reach the supplier's minimum. This can also cut down the cost of sewing because your seamstress doesn't have to change thread. But there's a catch: your thread must also be dye-able; if not, you must choose a thread color that will work with every color that your garments will be dyed in.

Is fabric readily available and how quickly can you reorder it? If there is a long waiting period or if the fabric is an <u>end lot</u>, you might want to rethink your choice or use another company as a backup for sourcing.

What is the minimum amount of fabric you should buy? Buy enough for at least three prototypes, plus one yard for testing. The prototypes can be used for marketing purposes—one for photographing, one for your sales rep, and one extra for any last minute needs (or in case of emergency).

Testing

You will need to test the fabric for shrinkage as well as for dye-ability if you plan to dye your garments. If you are garment dying, send samples of the fabric to the dye house for color matching. To determine shrinkage, cut one yard, measure it exactly, wash it, and dry it. Re-measure it. The difference, if any, will help you account for shrinkage in the pattern. You will also need to put appropriate care instructions on your finished garment, and this is a good starting point. Some knits should be <u>relaxed</u> before cutting, because the grain may be off, or it may be stretched when the fabric is rolled up tight. Your knits will need to be relaxed for about 48 hours before cutting. Your cutter will probably charge you extra to relax the fabric. Finding the right suppliers can be darn right daunting. In this example, Jenny explains the challenges she faced as a small business dealing with the big guys.

Real World Example

Designer: Jenny Hwa

Company: Loyale Clothing, www.loyaleclothing.com

Our biggest challenge was finding reliable vendors for fabrics, pattern making, and cutting/sewing production. Many companies did not aspire to work with a small company, so minimums were always an issue. The ones who would take on our business did not respect us enough to give us any priority or quality.

I found that the best solution was to do research, follow my gut instinct, and maintain the utmost confidence in myself and my business endeavor.

1. I am constantly researching vendors so I am never stuck with just one person in my rolodex to depend upon. Whether it is fabric vendors, printers, or a sewing facility, I am always online looking for new options.

2. If someone rubs me the wrong way, or I get a strange feeling about a working relationship, I walk away, even if the person or company is highly recommended. My gut instinct is the one thing I have learned to rely on, from designing to business relationships. Each time I have gone against my instinct, it has hurt my business in the long run.

3. At times vendors were not always willing to work with my small venture, however, my enthusiasm and confidence were infectious, and I won them over. I made them feel confident that success was imminent for my business, which meant future business for them.

I have to be the biggest fan of my business. If not me, then who? My top recommendation to people launching their own fashion company: Have the faith and confidence in yourself and your vision! When times get tough, those are the attributes that will carry you through. Unfortunately, with fashion, one minute you are hot and the next moment you are not, so it is up to you to create your own solid foundation so you can ride the highs and lows.

Jenny founded Loyale in 2005 after working in the industry with names such as Kate Spade, Catherine Malandrino, Jill Stuart and Chaiken. Loyale, made exclusively of eco-friendly fabrics, can be found in over 50 stores nationally and internationally and has received high acclaim in the press.

Fabric/Trim Spec Sheet

		Fabric/Trim
Name		

Supplier
 	
    Address
 	
    Phone		

Price per yard		
Fabric Width		
Fabric Weight		
Colors Available		
Minimum Yardage		
Fabric Content		
Care Instructions		

Fabric/Trim Spec Sheet

		Fabric/Trim
Name		

Supplier
 	
    Address
 	
    Phone		

Price per yard		
Fabric Width		
Fabric Weight		
Colors Available		
Minimum Yardage		
Fabric Content		
Care Instructions		

Chapter 12
Patterns and Samples

Everyone and their uncle is a patternmaker these days, so how do you find a good one? Through services such as 24seventalent.com, local design school employment offices or even Craigslist.org.

Let's start by discussing qualifications and experience. Some pattern drafters may take on projects they may not be inexperienced with. You could end up paying for their learning experience. But don't be afraid to work with a new person. You could discover an excellent patternmaker who doesn't yet charge like the pros. Here are a few questions to ask. (For the sake of simplicity, I use the female gender pronoun, but you are just as likely to encounter a male.)

- **How long have they been making patterns?** Experience counts, but having a newcomer isn't necessarily bad. All pattern makers have to start somewhere. Decide if experience is what you need for this particular project. If the person is new to the industry, their prices should reflect it.

- **What is their pattern specialty? Do they work with knits, wovens, or both?** Pattern drafting for each fabric type is very different, so you need to know what their experience is with each.

Resources for Freelancers:
24seventalent.com, guru.com, craigslist.org

Notes:

Notes:

- **Have they worked with one of your competitors?** If they have worked with a design line similar to yours, that may be a plus.

- **Can they give you client references?** This is a great way to find out how they work before your initial consultation.

- **Do they charge by the project or by the hour?** If it is a project price, find out how many samples are included in the price and what will additional samples cost over the project price.

- **Do they charge for consultations?**

- **Do they have a minimum charge?**

- **What is their turnaround time and do they charge extra for rush projects?**

If you find a patternmaker who does not do samples, get a referral from her for a sample maker. Finding an individual who does both is oftentimes better because she can translate the pattern into the most practical construction methods and can modify the patterns according to the production method needed.

Don't expect to get a perfect sample on your first try. If you do, this person is a keeper and please pass her information on to me; I would like to hire her. More commonly, expect the first sample to need revisions and don't expect it to be sewn at 100% quality. You are aiming for fit and are testing the initial design with the first sample. Your second and third sample should fit well, but you may still need revisions. If you can't get a good working sample by the fourth go, you might want to find another patternmaker. It's OK to shop around. If you have a few items, test out a couple individuals with different projects.

Preparing for your patternmaker

Before you meet with your patternmaker, determine for yourself how you would like your sizing and your fit. For example, is there a particular brand already available, in which their fit and sizing impresses you? This is a great starting point. Have sketches or pictures of similar designs and bring them to your first meeting. You should have your fabrics chosen at this point and have a small quantity of the fabric available for your samples. It is important to create your sample in the fabric you're going to use. Each fabric works differently. An inexpensive substitute is sometimes suitable.

At the end of your consultation, the patternmaker should give you a ballpark figure for two to three samples. If there are numerous unplanned changes in the design and fit between each sample phase, this would not be accounted for in the quote and you should expect to pay for it. Disorganization on your part can cause frustration for the patternmaker and will cost you. She will basically be starting over each time, doubling her time and your cost. Most seasoned patternmakers will overshoot the quote they give you for that reason. Treat your patternmaker as another professional, respecting her time and labor. If all goes well, the last sewn sample that she presents to you should be of production quality.

Notes:

_____

_____

_____

_____

_____

_____

_____

_____

_____

Recommended Reading:
An Entrepreneurs Guide to Sewn Product Manufacturing by Kathleen Fasanella

Chapter 13
Grading

Pattern. Check. Samples. Check. What's next in line? Grading. Grading refers to graduated sizes. In other words, you need to create a size range out of your pattern. Your patternmaker may be experienced in grading patterns, but the costs will add up quickly. A cheaper alternative is digital pattern grading. The price is usually per pattern piece and will cost pennies to what your patternmaker will charge.

Computerized grading, however, is not always the most accurate. If you get your garments graded digitally, I highly recommend creating a sample in each size. It doesn't have to be a pretty sample. You just need to make sure it fits your targeted sizes. If you are working in foundation clothing such as bras and underwear, you will need to find a specialist in grading these items to create grading rules for all your future designs.

Grading rules are a set measurement between sizes. Your grading rules will vary depending on whether you use knits or wovens and will also vary depending on your market and size range. For example, plus sizes use very different grading rules than missy sizes. The larger the sizes go in plus sizes, the greater the difference becomes. Missy sizing on the other hand,

Grading:
The size range of the garments. This is expressed by a numerical standard. For example, small/medium/large numerical standards will differ from the 2/4/6/8/10/12 size range.

Grading Rules:
The percentage and standard of change between each clothing size. Mathematical calculations are used to create proper grading rules.

Notes:
_____
_____
_____
_____
_____
_____

Notes:

is usually consistent between sizes. All these are things that you can ask your patternmaker to help you with. There are also books entirely on grading, so read them, or seek a professional to do the work for you.

After the process of developing your patterns and grading, you need to create garment specification sheets (or spec sheet for short). A spec sheet details everything about your garment in terms of finished measurements and sizes. Your patternmaker should be able to assist you in creating one. It details the finished measurements of each part of the garment for each size available.

Technical Sketch or Flat Sketch: An illustration of a garment with finished dimensions including all sewing details, seam lines and garment finishings.

The spec sheet also contains a detailed technical sketch as a reference for sewing. The technical sketch is usually created by the designer on a computer program such as Adobe Illustrator. For those of us that went to design school before this type of programs existed, a technical sketch may also be done by hand. A technical designer can assist you in developing a technical flat sketch.

A spec sheet helps each person in the process of production to understand the expectations of your finished garment through measurements and stitch lines.

This is an example of a spec sheet similar to one I use in my business. Please note that your spec sheet should be customized to accommodate your own business needs.

Grading   65

Spec Sheet

Date:	
Season:	
Style #:	
Style Name:	
Size Range:	
Yardage:	

Technical Flat

Measurements	Sizes						
	XS/2	S/4	M/6	L/8	XL/10	12	14

Spec Sheet

Date:	June 22, 2008
Season:	Basic: All Seasons
Style #:	1041
Style Name:	Bamboo Boyshorts
Size Range:	XS, S, M, L, XL
Yardage:	0.20

Technical Flat

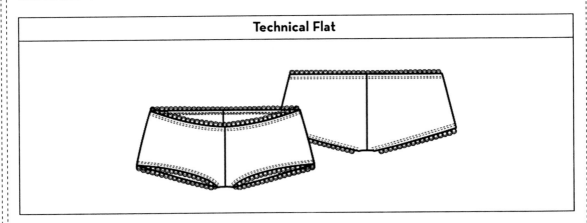

Measurements	Sizes						
	XS/2	S/4	M/6	L/8	XL/10	12	14
Waist Circumference	25"	26"	28"	30"	33"		
Leg Circumference	18"	19"	20"	21"	22 1/2"		
Side Seam	2 1/2"	3 1/2"	4 1/2"	6"	8"		
Center Front Height	5"	5 1/2"	6 1/2"	7 1/2"	9		
Center Back Height	7 1/2"	7 1/2"	8 1/2"	8 1/2"	9 1/2"		
Crotch width	2 1/2"	2 1/2"	2 1/2"	2 1/2"	2 1/2"		

Chapter 14
Cutting

You are one step closer to production when you reach the stage of cutting. Cutting is not as straightforward as pulling out a pair of dressmaker shears and chopping away at some fabric. The patterns must arrive at the cutters organized and prepped on a <u>marker</u>.

If you had your patterns digitally sized you are ahead of the game. If you had a pattern maker size your patterns, you will most likely need to get them digitized now. The reason? Many of the cutting services have grown with technology and now create digital markers for cutting various widths and lengths of fabrics. One advantage of digitized patterns is that they can be emailed, saving you the hassle of delivery.

Digital markers are a great advancement in the garment industry and your savior in figuring out how many garments you can create from your yardage. Why would a company prefer to do markers digitally rather than manually? To do it manually, you will have to lay out the pattern pieces by eye and trace them off by hand. With digital markers, the computer creates the layout automatically, depending on the width of fabric – saving you both time and material.

Marker: a paper representation of all pattern pieces to determine how many garments can be cut from the fabric with the least amount of waste.

Notes:

Fabric Width: *Different fabrics come in different widths. The norm is between 45" and 60" wide.*

For costing purposes discussed later in Chapter 41, you can use a marker and the <u>fabric width</u> to determine the exact amount of fabric needed for one garment. You can get help from your patternmaker to get an accurate amount.

Notes:

_____

_____

_____

_____

_____

_____

_____

_____

_____

_____

In order to make sure you are allowing for enough fabric in your costing, have your patternmaker take into consideration all sizes in which you plan to make the garment and calculate the average amount of fabric used per garment. Use this amount in Chapter 41, Variable Costs.

Your cutters may sometimes also be your production contractors, so you may not need to worry as much about cutting being a separate step. Some cutters may also offer grading, marking, and digitizing. A company that offers cutting, sewing and all of these pattern services under one roof is referred to as being vertically integrated, or as CMT (cut, make, trim).

Minimum Cut Charge: *the minimum charge to cut any quantity of fabric.*

If you are shopping around for cutting services, get two or more quotes for different quantities. Find out what the <u>minimum cut charge</u> is. Use the higher quote for costing purposes in Chapter 41. You will need to know how many pattern pieces are in each garment for your quote to be accurate.

Be clear when working with a cutting service by providing a detailed cut sheet for each garment. The cut sheet details the fabrics and pattern pieces that need to be cut for each garment, as well as the technical flat for reference.

This is an example of a cut sheet similar to one I use in my business. Please note that your cut sheet should be customized to accommodate your own business needs.

Cut Sheet

Date:	
Season:	
Style #:	
Style Name:	
Size Range:	
Yardage:	

Technical Flat	Swatches
	SELF
	LINING
	INTERFACING

Pattern Pieces

SELF	FACING	INTERFACING	

Quantity

Colorways	Sizes						
	XS/2	S/4	M/6	L/8	XL/10	12	14
Total							

This is an example of how one might fill out a cut sheet. This should contain actual swatches of your fabrics and trims that will be cut. Please note that your cut sheet should be customized to accommodate your own business needs.

Cut Sheet

Date:	June 22, 2008
Season:	Spring 2009
Style #:	2064
Style Name:	Bamboo Tank Top
Size Range:	S, M, L
Yardage:	0.65

Technical Flat	Swatches
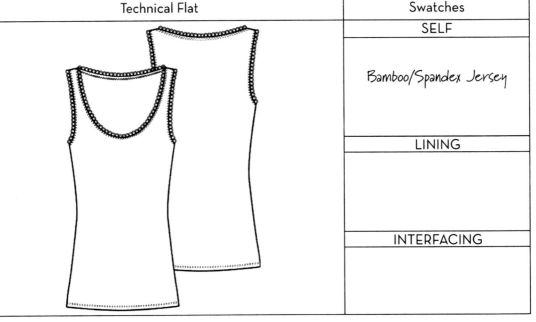	**SELF** Bamboo/Spandex Jersey **LINING** **INTERFACING**

Pattern Pieces

SELF	FACING	INTERFACING	
1 Tank Front			
1 Tank Back			

Quantity

Colorways	Sizes						
	XS/2	S/4	M/6	L/8	XL/10	12	14
Red	5	10	20	10	5		
Blue	5	10	20	10	5		
Green	5	10	20	10	5		
White	5	10	20	10	5		
Total	20	40	80	40	20		

Chapter 15
Production

We are down to the last step in getting your product made—the actual production of your garment. You have screened your patternmaker and sample maker. Now you need to screen your sewing contractors.

Not every contractor will work for you, and the referrals you get may not always pan out. You should know, from your final samples, what types of machines are needed to produce your garment. Not every sewing contractor has every specialty machine. Buttonhole, zig-zag, blind hem, flat lock, or rolled hem machines are special equipment that may not be in every contractor's inventory. Know what you need before settling on a contractor.

Don't limit yourself to one contactor either. Try a few until you get one that will work well with you. Follow your instincts. I tried three before I settled on the one I currently use.

My present contractors and I have a mutual respect for each other and our relationship has grown with my business. They were willing to work with me and my deadlines. I went from being *very* disorganized to giving them everything bundled

Notes:

Production Card:
A chart that includes a technical flat of the finished garment, trims to be used, pattern pieces, finished measurements, and construction details.

Notes:
_____
_____
_____
_____
_____
_____
_____
_____
_____
_____
_____
_____
_____
_____
_____
_____
_____

properly with swatches and specs. When I began working with them, I don't think I had a properly sewn sample, let alone a <u>production</u> <u>card</u> to go with the garments. They walked me through it all. I still forget to drop things off at times, but they respect me enough not to put me on the back burner, and we continue to meet my deadlines. This trust and recognition came with time. The first production they did for me was not that great, but as I stuck with them and communicated my expectations, my production became more efficient and of a higher quality.

When choosing your contractors, see how much work they have lying around. If it looks like they are busy, ask if you will get the priority you need. Get price quotes. Have realistic ideas of how much you want to spend on each piece. The per-piece price is usually negotiable, but don't insult them. They have to make a living too and recognizing this will help develop mutual respect. You will oftentimes get better prices if your production is larger.

There are listings of sewing contractors in the printed and online version of the Business-to-Business yellow pages. Call around, ask questions. Not every factory has English speaking laborers, so make sure there is someone you can communicate with. Language barriers are sometimes a problem.

Finding the right factory for your production takes patience. In the next case study, Julie describes how she found answers to her production challenges.

Real World Example

Designer: Julie Busch

Company Description: Buhl Company Inc., www.buhlzone.com

Finding the right factory for each garment type is extremely important if you want to achieve the quality you expect for your brand and the price point you hope to reach. My biggest challenge was finding the right people to sew my garments—from samples to production. With the manufacturing trending to Asia and Latin America in the recent decade, it was, and still is, difficult to find the right factory for each garment. As a 20-year veteran in the corporate services industry, I had very little experience in the garment business and not a single contact.

To overcome the problem, I started networking with anyone I could find in the business, and quickly found two professionals who could provide insight into the local garment and factory scene. We found a sample maker who helped for the first two seasons, but we quickly outgrew her capacity. We found a new sample maker through another person who joined our team.

As for factories, it appeared that they were just a shadow of what used to be here. We contracted with one factory in the U.S. to sew our first production run in Fall '07, but they were not a good fit. Through a referral, we started working with two large and well established factories. We have invested much time into getting these factories up to speed on producing our garments, but it remains an uphill challenge, particularly as we introduce new fabrics and styles. Our next biggest challenge comes from the fact that our factories are getting busier as manufacturing gradually moves back to the U.S.

Finding the right production facility takes a lot of patience, as it is an ongoing process to keep up with the constant changes in the industry.

Julie Busch formed The Buhl Company, Inc. in 2006 after working in market research for the apparel, automotive and technology industries.

This is an example of a production pattern card similar to one I use in my business. This is very similar to a cut sheet, with additional information. Please note that your production pattern card should be customized to accommodate your own business needs.

Production Pattern Card

Date:	
Season:	
Style #:	
Style Name:	
Size Range:	
Delivery:	
Contractor	

Technical Flat	Swatches
	SELF
	FACING
	INTERFACING

Pattern Pieces

SELF	FACING	INTERFACING	

Quantity

Colorways	Sizes						
	XS/2	S/4	M/6	L/8	XL/10	12	14

Packing Method:		Hang Tag:	

Construction Details:

This is an example of how one might fill out a production pattern card. This should include swatches of your fabric and all trims used in production. Please note that your production pattern card should be customized to accommodate your own business needs.

Production 75

Production Pattern Card

Date:	June 22, 2008
Season:	Fall 2008
Style #:	3085
Style Name:	Bamboo Tee Shirt
Size Range:	S, M, L
Delivery:	August 1, 2008
Contractor:	ABC Sewing

Technical Flat	Swatches
	SELF
	FACING
	INTERFACING

Pattern Pieces

SELF	FACING	INTERFACING	
Tee Front			
Tee Back			
Right Sleeve			
Left Sleeve			
Neck Binding			

Quantity

	Sizes						
Colorways	XS/2	S/4	M/6	L/8	XL/10	12	14
Red	5	10	20	10	5		
Blue	5	10	20	10	5		
Green	5	10	20	10	5		
White	5	10	20	10	5		

Packing Method:		Hang Tag:	

Construction Details: Overlock all seams, Sleeve Hem Coverstitch 1/2", Shirt Hem Coverstitch 1"

A Look into International Manufacturing

Interview with Shveta Shourie, Designer & Business Owner, Shveta Shourie, www.shvetashourie.com

Where do you contract and how did you find your overseas factory?

I presently manufacture in India. I originally looked to family friends in the industry, but later used referrals to find my current manufacturers. There are websites that can help in the search, such as Tradekey.com or HKTDC.com. They list thousands of manufacturers from over 220 countries.

If you use the website approach, how do you weed through all the companies?

I narrowed them down by product. Some of the manufacturers on these sites will just supply you with their own garments, but some are willing to work with you through the process of developing your own products.

How many companies have you worked with?

I have worked with three suppliers and I personally interviewed them and took a tour of their factories in India. It makes sense to work with two or three manufacturers at the same time so that you ensure a timely delivery from at least one. You should not completely rely on one vendor.

Do they source everything for you?

Yes, they sourced everything. If you have a large enough order or you meet certain minimums, they will even weave and print the fabric that you desire for your collection. This saves money for both the contractor and the designer. They can even produce trims and buttons for you in their factory if the order is large enough. For smaller orders, they will buy what you need from the market, though it may not be the exact same quality you were planning for your collection.

How is your quality control handled?

Normally they have a quality control officer in their factory but I would highly recommend having someone from your team there to check all pieces in the shipment before they leave the factory, or have someone on this end do it. This person should also make sure that the packaging of every piece is done according to your specifications.

What minimums must you have to manufacture overseas?

Minimums can vary from 25 to 10,000. For me, smaller runs have turned into a costly experience. The per piece price can decrease significantly as you increase your quantities. Of course, with all the added expenses for international manufacturing, it really only makes sense if you have larger quantities.

What are some of the costs associated with manufacturing internationally?

If this is your first time, you want to go and meet up with the manufacturers and take a tour of their facility. Cost of travel, airfare, accommodation, international phone calls and fax, sampling and production are the major costs. If you are not there personally, you will have to hire a quality control person which is an additional cost but can make your life easier. On top of this, do not forget to add the cost of shipping and handling, customs duty, and storage rental once your shipment is here. I would also suggest hiring a customs broker to help with all the legalities and to make everything run smoothly.

How do you deal with customs, do you need an agent?

It is imperative that you take this seriously. You should hire a customs broker. Do some research and find out who has already dealt in apparel and other fashion accessories. It is important to find out if the agent or the agency has worked with the suppliers and manufacturers from the country you are doing business with. They would have a better idea of what the customs regulations and quotas for that country are. Quotas refer to the maximum amount of a specific product that can be exported to the U.S. from that country. They are different for each country. There is a "most favored nations" status given to some countries and for those, customs duty may be lower. Your agent will be able to advise you on all the specifics. You may also contact the consulate for the country you plan on doing business with to find an appropriate agent that way.

How long does it take from completing a sample to a complete product?

Finding the right manufacturer(s) can take a long time. But once you are past that step, the whole process can take up to six to seven months. Sampling may take one to two months. You want to get samples in your hot little hands as soon as possible to approve them. Production can take another three months (sometimes less). If you want to have a positive profit margin, you should consider receiving your shipment by sea which can take another two to three months, but it is very cost effective. If you are pressed for time, you can get it by courier (by air of course) but you will end up paying three to four times more. This can be very costly if your shipment is large.

I know there are concerns about international factories stealing designs and producing them before producing yours. How can you avoid this?

You should ask the factory to sign an agreement that they will not reproduce this design. The agreement is usually valid for one and a half years.

What would you recommend for payment arrangements?

I would suggest a Letter of Credit rather than a wire transfer. With wire transactions, you pay the exporter without verifying that all of your guidelines have been followed in packing and shipping your products. You could get stuck with something damaged or something you didn't even order. A Letter of Credit (LC) will make sure that if there is any damage to your shipment or the quality is poor, the exporter does not get paid. I would recommend doing some research on which terms and conditions should be a part of your LC and use it as a source of payment for your transactions. I would recommend you have your lawyer set up the LC and assist in facilitating the transfer.

be a part of your LC and use it as a source of payment for your transactions. I would recommend you have your lawyer set up the LC and assist in facilitating the transfer.

If someone is seriously considering international sourcing, what can you recommend to them?
Hire an agent or liaison to work with the international sourcing. It will not be cheap, but you will save yourself a lot of headaches. There are international trade shows for manufacturers that you can attend. This is ideal, because you really would want to talk to them in person. Infomat.com has lists of all the trade shows in this arena.

Fairtradeusa.org – Certifies fair trade organizations and advises companies on how to implement fair trade in manufacturing.

Chapter 16
The Green Movement

The buzz words "green" and "sustainable" seem to apply to everything these days, but what do they actually mean? A "green" business is not as simple as just a one sentence definition, because the word itself could cover and pertain to so many different things.

While many industries have certification standards and programs with regards to environmental sustainability, certification for the garment industry does not yet exist. Some cities and states have initiated their own certification programs, which can vary in cost from free to $5,000 per year. The majority of the programs are offered by privately held, for-profit companies. The expense makes it less likely for fabric suppliers and sewing contractors to seek a green certification, especially since the benefit rarely translates into tangible profits. This may change in the future, but as of now, it's the reality. However, that doesn't mean you can't do your part to try and limit your business's footprint on the environment.

Supporting local businesses and local manufacturing creates a sustainable economy, in the sense that it maintains wealth within your own community. Sustainable also means longevity

Notes:

Notes:

The Green Guide (www.thegreenguide.com) has detailed information on green fabrics that are available.

Recommended Reading:
"Sustainable Fashion" published by Fairchild Publications.

and certain fabrics can be described as such in that they last longer and therefore use less resources to grow or manufacture. Any effort to reduce use of resources such as sourcing locally instead of having materials shipped from a far off land, promotes sustainability.

Organic is different from sustainable, and describes a product that has been grown without pesticides, genetically changed organisms, or synthetic fertilizers. A fabric can be certified as organic by the United States Department of Agriculture.

Fabrics have come a long way in the last few years. It seems nowadays that everything can become a fabric. Bamboo, soybean, cornstalk, hemp, and recycled polyester have all become new, "green" choices in fabrics. (Who knows, maybe we'll one day see fabric made from hair or toenail clippings.) Educate yourself on the qualities of the fabrics you plan on using. You too can take advantage of the "green" movement.

Although many designers are already opting for the "green" route in their businesses, retailers and shoppers have not traveled as fast on the eco-conscious train as designers have. To most shoppers, price is still the determining factor; the fact that a garment is eco-friendly is a bonus, but what really matters is their bank account. Do some research to find out if your customer is one that would spend money on "green" clothing lines.

MARKETING

Chapter 17
Introduction to Marketing

How does the world find out about you? Through the mighty wonders of marketing. Marketing sounds like a mysterious universe that everybody but you knows about. You might be surprised how much you actually know. Independent designers typically overlook this segment of the business, but it is marketing that yields the most importance in building your design business.

Marketing is the process of getting your name, brand and product out in the marketplace. It is an extension of branding and a bridge to sales. How might one achieve successful marketing? For independent designers, the most common way is through press releases, email marketing campaigns, and personal and online networking.

Notes:

Chapter 18
Press Releases

Press Releases are the most popular way of getting the word out to the press about your business happenings. I will first discuss how to write one and then how to distribute it.

How to Write a Press Release

Press releases are written as news articles and are used to announce a newsworthy business event. Before you spend your time and money on a release, make sure your news is important. Not everything is news. Newsworthy stories include business launches, new products, and special business events. Announcing an ordinary event, such as a 20% off sale, is not really worthy of a press release.

A good release will answer the questions who, what, where, when, why, and how. Your headline and first paragraph should summarize your story. It is sometimes easier to write this part last. The rest of your article should provide all the details.

Think of who you want to be interested in the story—this is your audience—then focus on the news that is relevant to them. Use an active voice and strong verbs. Most releases are under 500 words and some companies require that releases are fewer

Notes:

Notes:

New Release services:
prnewswire.com,
businesswire.com

than 400 words, so make every word count. Include opinions as direct quotes, otherwise, use facts. Your release should conclude with a short paragraph about your company history, products, and services.

Many distribution channels distribute your releases by headline and summary only, so be sure to prepare a one-paragraph summary.

Make sure your article is brief and to the point. We are bombarded with news these days – the faster you can give the details, the more grateful your readers will be!

Distribution of your Press Release
There are a several ways you can distribute your press release. The most expensive way is to use a Public Relations (PR) firm to send out your release. One step down is to use the actual services that the PR firm submits your press release to.

Two of the largest online distribution channels are BusinessWire.com and PRNewsWire.com. Their news distribution is over 10 times larger than the less expensive companies or those that offer free distribution. This is one area where going with the cheaper option may cost you. If you are going to invest time and effort in writing a press release, you should make the investment on the distribution service.

Prices for services can range up to $500 per release, so this makes it even more important to submit a thorough, specific, and timely release. There are many companies that offer writing services—if you are not sure about your writing abilities, this might be a time to hire one.

Another way to submit s press release is to send it directly to the press outlets that you want to cover your business. If you contact them directly, make sure to follow up afterwards. If using email, send the release in the body of the email, not as an attachment. Most publications have contact info for editors on their websites. You can search for them yourself, or get an intern to compile a contact list for you.

Press Release Template

The Headline Announces Your News
The summary paragraph summarizes the news being presented in the full release. Many readers will decide from the summary paragraph whether they will continue to the remainder of the release. Keep this under four sentences.

City, State, Date — The lead sentence contains the most important information in your release. Grab your reader's attention here by stating the news you have to announce. Do not assume that your reader has read your headline or summary paragraph.

A news release is like a news story. Keep your sentences and paragraphs short, about three or four lines per paragraph. The first couple of paragraphs should answer who, what, when, where, why and how.

The standard press release is 300 to 600 words. Topics for a press release can include announcements of new products, the publishing of a book or the launch of a new business.

"Adding a quote to provide editorial content is acceptable," said lama Coolcat. "You can convey biased information in a quote that you can't include in the rest of the release."

Conclude your press release with a little background on you, your company and your products.

Contact Information:
Joe Smith
Your Cool Company
Phone number
Website

Press Release Example

afterglow **Design Studio Moves to Oakland's Chinatown**

*Oakland boutique, **afterglow**, closes its Temescal doors to open a new design studio and showroom in Oakland's Chinatown. Amy M. Cools, the mastermind of **afterglow** is the designer behind the unique stylings of AC Clothing and Bags.*

Oakland, California, January 20th, 2008 – After almost two years of providing a creative shopping experience in Oakland's Temescal neighborhood, the *afterglow* boutique closed it's retail doors this January to open a design studio and showroom in Oakland's Chinatown.

afterglow has been showcasing independent designer collections since it's inception in July 2006 with a focus on California bay area artists. Afterglow was originally started as an outlet for designer Amy M. Cools to showcase her collection and line, AC Clothing and Bags, but soon developed into a destination for shoppers, artists and the like.

Designer Amy M. Cools offered "I love supporting other artists and designers, although I need to refocus my attention on my true vision for *afterglow*, a showroom for AC Clothing and Bags." In late December 2008, Cools made the decision to close her retail location and open an independent design studio and showroom.

The *afterglow* studio is nearly twice the space as her Temescal location, and is now open by appointment and for special events. This new location has provided Cools with new opportunities to grow her clothing and accessories line. She has added several limited-edition and one-of-a-kind designs under her label and has resumed her work in the community.

Cools first introduced her unique collection in Southern California over ten years ago. Her designs are inspired by the bright and playful vintage fabrics she acquires. Although Cools has refocused her direction on her design aspirations, she still remains an active member in promoting local artists, designers and boutiques. Her side project, *afterglow*'s Guide to Independent California Shopping, supports and showcases her colleagues, as well as other amazing independent designers.

The AC Clothing and Bags collection can be sought at various boutiques across the US as well as online through Etsy.com. For more information on *afterglow*'s Guide to Independent California Shopping and AC Clothing and Bags, log onto www.acclothingandbags.com.

Contact Information:
Amy M. Cools
afterglow Design Studio and Showroom
261 10th St, Suite 202
Oakland, California, 94607
(510) 654-7514
amy@acclothingandbags.com
www.acafterglow.etsy.com

Chapter 19
Email Marketing Campaigns

Email marketing is a great tool to help grow your business. Companies such as Constant Contact and Vertical Response offer services that can help you organize and design your email marketing campaign. These services also offer tools for tracking how many people open your email and how soon after you send it that it is opened. You can use this information to fine tune and sharpen your email campaigns.

Email Marketing Services: *verticalresponse.com, constantcontact.com, icontact.com*

These companies do not sell email lists. In fact, selling or buying an email list is illegal and the Can-Spam Act prohibits it. You are responsible for growing your email list yourself. One way to do this is to add an email sign up box to your website. These services allow you to use the list you've generated to send out professional looking company announcements.

Can-Spam Act of 2003: *Requires an unsubscribe option, the subject to relate to the context of an email, and a physical address for the email sender. This act prohibits the harvesting or selling of email lists.*

Be sure to keep the email addresses you collect private. This information is proprietary and it is illegal to share it without permission.

From my own personal experiences with email marketing, I have a few secrets to share. I schedule my emails to go out between 9:30 and 10:30 in the morning on weekdays. Before that time, they could get lost in somebody's inbox and spam; after that, the person might be working hard and may not get the opportunity to read them. Sending my emails at this time keeps them fresh in my customers' inboxes while they are responding to the previous day's emails. The day you send your emails out also matters. Is the email for an event on Friday? Send it out on Wednesday when people are planning out their weekends. Is it for a sale on your website? Send it out on payday. You can design your emails days in advance and schedule the time for release accordingly.

Email Campaign Etiquette

Take this bit of advice from an email campaign savvy entrepreneur.

There's a good change your name is part of an email list, and probably more than one. Some we signed up for voluntarily and others we just ended up on one way or another.

How do you end up on an unwanted email list? Easy. We all get them, the emails from a friend or colleague who sends an email to a large group of people and places all recipients in the "To" box or the "CC" box.

Yep, you know what I mean and you have probably done it too. I've been guilty of sending a simple email to a group of friends asking about the best restaurant or inviting them to an event with everybody openly cc'd. With friends, it not a big deal.

Where things can get problematic is if you send an email promotion of your business or an event with an open line of contact information for a large number of people you know vaguely or not at all, such as customers who signed your email list. All it takes is for one person on that list to say "hey, this is free information and I'm taking it," and start spamming your list with their promotions. It happens.

This is not only unethical but illegal. It's stealing someone's proprietary information without their consent and it is punishable by law. What's the law? This is the classic definition of spamming.

Can you avoid having your name used that way? Not really. The best thing you can do is to remember that there is a hidden box in emails labeled "BCC" for blind carbon copy. Make a habit of using it or you could someday send out an email, someone on your open list could be having a bad day, could be working at a law firm, and the rest is history. You could find yourself having a bad day too.

Chapter 20
Creating a Web Presence

Everybody's on the web these days, whether they have something to say or something to sell. Truth be told, your business will not be taken seriously without a website.

There are two main ways you can create your website. One is the traditional way using HTML code with or without the help of a web designer. The second, and increasingly popular, way to get a website quickly is through templates provided by sites such as Yahoo.com or Blogger.com. I will get into blogging in the next chapter, but just so you are aware, it is an option for web design as well.

If you are going the traditional route, you need to figure out what kind of website you need. Look to other sites that sell products similar to yours. What navigation do they have? Do you need the same or better navigation? Do you need an online store where your customers can buy directly from you or will you be marketing via your website to a wholesale market?

Notes:

Notes:

Prepare all the information you'll want on your website before meeting with your web designer. Compile your bio, your company information, your services, products, wholesale information, links you want to include, and anything else you can think of prior to your meeting. Get all your images ready (give your images recognizable names: "pillow.jpg", not "image22.jpg"). Have ideas about a color scheme. It should be consistent with your branding.

If you chose the template route, you are more limited in your layout, and for the most part, your site will look home-made. Think of your customer. If you do not plan on taking your company into the mainstream eye, a template may be the desired look for you, but if you do, your site should be customized to meet this market.

Search Engine Optimization

Information on Search Engine Optimization (SEO) provided by SEO expert Elizabeth Sullivan,

The most beautifully designed website would be worth zilch if your customers can't find it. How do you ensure that your website shows up in search engines? Here are a few simple tricks to help you out.

Notes:

Search Engine Optimization (SEO) is what web designers call the little tweaks you do to make your website easy for search engines such as Google and Yahoo to find.

• Make sure your page titles are descriptive and contain your business name. Limit your title to 60 characters.

• Make sure your website has page descriptions. Your descriptions will appear in the search engines along with your page titles and will be your first selling point with those browsing for info. Limit your description to 150 characters.

- Use key word phrases (e.g., empire waist dress) rather than just key words (e.g. dress). Limit your key word phrases to 10.

Just one more tip for a better website:
- Hire a professional to do all this if you feel it's too much for you to deal with.

Hot Tip!

If you are unsure what keywords to include, search the engines for the products that you want your website to come up on. Look at the top sites and take a peek at their source code. All browsers have a menu command for viewing the source code. Scroll down on the source code page to see what the page's keywords are. Use this as a guide for developing your own key words and phrases. Do not copy another site's keywords, word for word; this would be plagiarism. More importantly, do not use your competitor's name in your keywords; if the name is trademarked, you could be in for a lawsuit.

Notes:

Chapter 21
Blogging

It's so easy to do, my grandfather is even doing it. What might you ask? Blogging. With very little or no web knowledge, anyone can post their latest news online. Many companies have abandoned traditional websites to use a blog as their main web presence.

Why would someone prefer to host a blog as opposed to a website? Blogs often show up higher in search engines because they are updated regularly. Many companies use blogs as either their main website or as part of it to provide regular updates about their products. Here is a little article about blogging by our blog expert Lorraine Sanders, explaining the basics of this popular new medium.

Notes:

A Little Blog Know How

By Lorraine Sanders, author of SFIndieFashion.com

Don't think of your company's blog as just an online journal. Instead, look at it as a catalog, public relations maven, branding pro, marketing diva, and never-ending networking event that's working 24-7 to get your voice, your products, and your message out into the world. Better yet, it's free—and you are in complete control of it.

Whether you chronicle the trials and tribulations of a hectic production cycle, post images of fabric swatches and sketches to preview upcoming collections, or highlight your company's latest news and events, maintaining a blog allows you to show fellow bloggers, fashion journalists, shop owners, and customers a side of your company that would otherwise remain hidden.

The beauty of blogging is that it works both ways. It allows you to broadcast your message outward, but it also pulls people in, and that increases your chances of being discovered by more and more people.

When you blog, you create an ever-growing series of pathways for people to find you through search engine results, RSS subscriptions, other blogs and their blogrolls, or favorite links lists. Of course, building relationships in the blogosphere doesn't happen overnight – or without an ongoing effort to reach out to other bloggers. But over time, you're likely to find that your company's blog has paved the way for new relationships with fellow designers, journalists, retail buyers, and everyday customers.

Ready to blog? When you're ready to get started, you can easily set up a free blog using the templates of Blogger.com or WordPress.com. If you want a look that's integrated with your company's existing web site, and you don't know how to do that on your own, save yourself the headache and hire a professional to do it for you. Don't forget to look at other blogs for inspiration, and add your favorites to your blogroll (don't forget to ask them to reciprocate). You're ready to start posting. See you in the blogosphere.

Five Habits of Successful Bloggers

The most successful bloggers:

• Blog often.

• Read other blogs as often as their own.

• Have a consistent point of view.

• Know the power of a good photograph or image.

• Network like mad, online and off.

Five Sites Every Blogger Should Know and Love

1. Technorati

2. BlogCatalog

3. BlogHop

4. ProBlogger

5. Blogged

What Does That Mean?! Weird Blogging Words Defined.

RSS: Formally known as Really Simple Syndication, RSS technology allows anyone with a web site to syndicate content. In a nutshell, it allows you to make your blog posts available to anyone who subscribes to your feed using a program like Google Reader, NewsGator or Bloglines. In turn, you can use these programs to subscribe to other blogs. It's an easy, convenient way to receive content from all your favorite blogs in one place—instead of having to check multiple sites daily or wade through a slew of emails.

Tags: Tags are simply relevant keywords you choose and attach to your posts in order to help more readers find your blog and locate specific content once they're there. Tags can appear in "tag clouds", which are basically groups of keywords. Use a tag often, and the keyword in your tag cloud will grow larger in size relative to other tags you've used less often. Sites that monitor and search blogs – like Technorati –group blog posts from many blogs according to their tags in huge tag clouds. Tag a post with the word "fashion," for example, and your post will appear alongside other posts tagged with that word.

Pinging: When your blog pings another site or service, it is simply saying, in tech-speak, "Hey, I've updated my content." Most blogging platforms have pinging capabilities built in and notify blog search engines and blog directories every time you create new content.

Blogroll: A blogroll is really just a list of links to other blogs and web sites. Think of it as a list of favorites or friends. You can fill your blogroll with any site you choose, but most bloggers populate their blogrolls with blogs they read or want to endorse. Blogrolls will help you grow readership if you make a habit of asking other bloggers to reciprocate whenever you add a new blog to your blogroll.

Using Blogs Even Further

Not only is blogging great for you to do, but it is also great to be mentioned by one—especially if the blog has industry clout. Bloggers are often seen as the new journalists of our time. If a respected blogger mentions or recommends a product, that product could become highly demanded overnight. How might you get mentioned on someone's blog? Send the blogger an email introducing you and your product to them. Don't send them a press release; a blogger is a person, not a business—use a personal touch.

If you want your product mentioned (and who doesn't?), find out which blogs are read most frequently and which blogs your competitors are being mentioned on. You can do this by using blog search engines like Technorati.com or social bookmarking websites such as StumbleUpon.com or Digg.com. Once you find the blogs you want, subscribe to them and comment on them. The more you comment, the more likely those writers are to mention your product.

Chapter 22
Social Media

Social media is so vast, varied, and evolving that by the time this book is published there will likely be several dozen more social networks on the front. One of the first social networks I remember is Friendster.com. I used it to connect with friends and high school buddies.

These days social networking has taken a life of its own. No longer are we using these networks to only stay in touch with friends; instead, we're using them to promote businesses and products. Social media can not only connect you to potential customers, it is also a great way to network with other professionals in your area of expertise.

In fact, social media has become so common, that there are professionals who specialize in setting up and maintaining social networks for that purpose specifically.

Not all social media is suitable for each industry nor are they all relevant. You could spend countless hours searching through all the different networks. A few well known social sites for promoting fashion businesses are ETSY.com and Facebook. com, but there are dozens of others out there, so check

Based on an interview with Hazel Grace Dircksen, Social Internet Strategist, Social Bees Strategy, www.socialbeesstrategy. com

Notes:

Social media you should know about: etsy.com, facebook.com, haute.net, fashionindustrynetwork.com

around. If you are, or have children that are part of the Y generation, you probably know more about social networking than most entrepreneurs do, so you have an **advantage**. Hire yourself a professional if you need to, or get the neighbors' kids to help you.

Chapter 23
Networking

Of course, before blogging and social media came along, there was the traditional form of networking where people meet face to face. Networking is one of the most powerful tools you can use to grow your business. Networking can happen anywhere but the easiest way is by joining a group. There are industry-specific networking groups, entrepreneurial groups, gender-specific groups, and cultural groups. Try more than one group. I personally belong to two different networking groups: a fashion industry group and a women's entrepreneurial group.

To find a networking group of your interest, try Craigslist. org or Meetup.com. Both contain links to all kinds of groups. Many groups invite speakers on topics that may be relevant to your business. Chances are, at a talk or a meeting, you'll meet other professionals you can brainstorm with and share resources.

I joined a group over a year ago for women entrepreneurs called "Ladies Who Launch." I found it incredibly resourceful, not only in the topics they cover at meetings, but because it helped introduce me into a community of women whom I would have never had the opportunity to meet otherwise.

Notes:

They have proven to be a reliable and useful support group for when I needed them most.

Networking groups: *Meetup.com,* *ladieswholaunch.com,* *econnect.entreprenuer.* *com*

I also participate in a fashion industry networking group. This group has led to several media opportunities and partnerships that I might not have otherwise created. The group is attended not only by designers, but business owners, photographers, models, media, and everyone in between. Networking groups create an opportunity to be on the same playing field as others, whether you are a student or a professional.

Chapter 24
The Elevator Pitch

A useful skill to have down before attending a networking event is delivering your "elevator pitch". The elevator pitch is a 30-second pitch about what you do, why you do it, and why someone else would want to know more about you and your business.

Why the goofy name? It comes from the imaginary situation of being in the elevator at some undisclosed location when the editor of "The Coolest Magazine Ever" walks in. Are you going to let this opportunity cross your path and not take advantage of it? Of course not, you want to introduce yourself, give Ms. Hot Shot a card and make an unforgettable impression. You think this may never happen to you? Opportunity comes to those who are ready for it, so why not be ready?

What's a successful elevator pitch? Here are a few pointers:

• Be prepared. Always carry business cards, promotional fliers, or even your product around with you.

• Be 100% positive and always smile. Even if you are going through the nastiest divorce and are filing for bankruptcy, nobody has to know that but you. If you give the appearance

Notes:

Notes:

that everything is dandy, there will be no reason for the other person to feel awkward.

- Don't be overly intrusive but be inquisitive. Start the conversation. Have confidence and express an interest in the person. It will make a lasting impression. People love talking about themselves. Don't worry; you will get your turn. When it is your turn, be precise and succinct in your pitch.

- If you exchange business cards, follow up with an email or a call to say it was a pleasure to have met them. If the person was interested in your business, ask if he or she would like to join your mailing list. This could be a future customer.

Happy networking!

SALES AND PROMOTION

Chapter 25
Introduction to Sales

The question I hope you've thought about is, "How do I actually make money with my product?" It wouldn't make sense to have a business if you didn't, would it? If you are getting to this point and your reaction is "I don't care about the money," my recommendation is to band together with others who call themselves starving artists and move into a commune. For those who are more like, "Yes, I want to make money and live off of it," the following chapters are about selling your creations successfully.

Sales can be split into two categories: direct and indirect. Simply stated, some you have direct control over and some you don't. Starting with the obvious, selling directly to your customer is going to give you the highest profit margin. You act as the retailer in this situation. Whether you are selling online, at street fairs, or taking custom orders, you control your profit.

Notes:

- -

- -

- -

- -

- -

- -

- -

- -

- -

- -

- -

- -

- -

Chapter 26
Direct Sales

Internet Sales

Internet Sales are becoming the way of the future. In addition
to having a website to maximize your exposure, you can
now easily set up your own online store. There are several
companies who help promote independent artists and
designers through online stores. Etsy.com, SmashingDarling.
com, ShopFlick.com, and IndieDesignerLabels.com are just a
few examples. Another way to sell directly is through ebay.com,
although this has changed over the years and unless you are
selling at dirt cheap prices, you may just end up wasting time
going this route.

If you want to set yourself apart as a professional designer
label, you may consider hosting a webstore directly on your
website. There are several ways to do this. Some website
hosting companies also offer shopping carts, for example,
Prostores.com. The monthly charge is much higher than for
regular hosting. Another way is to purchase a ready made
shopping cart component and use it with your regular hosting
website. You maintain a low monthly charge, but you purchase
the shopping cart software outright.

*Online indie
shopping sites:* etsy.com,
smashingdarling.com,
shopflick.com,
indiedesignerlabels.com

Notes:

Notes:

Shopping cart software can cost anywhere from $100-$5,000, which is in addition to your web hosting and payment processing charges. Depending on the time you have and the amount of money you wish to spend on setting everything up, you have many options. Be realistic in assessing your ability to set up and manage your online store. If you are not computer savvy, I recommend you hire someone to tackle this for you.

Besides setting up your shopping cart, you will also need to set up payment processing on your site. Paypal.com is one option; although not the least expensive of all that is available, but it is the easiest to set up.

The obvious advantage of having an online store is that you have direct contact with your customers and receive immediate payments. The drawback is that you must keep merchandise inventory updated and ship out the orders as they are received. This requires a fair amount of organization. Again, if you are not that kind of person, or can't hire somebody to handle it, online sales may not be the best option for you.

Street fairs

Street fairs can be great fun. You enjoy 100% customer interaction and receive instant feedback on your merchandise. Street fairs are the fastest way to develop your sales skills. These sales skills will help you with pitching your product to stores, reps, and the media.

Most cities have craft and art fairs where vendor space is available. Contact your city or neighborhood associations for information on participating. Fees can range from $75-$1,500 depending on the event and the amount of promotion by the organizers.

Vendor space is also available at most jazz festivals, wine fairs, and music events. Keep in mind that while your audience at these events is everyone, most people will expect to pay a fairly small amount. Use street fairs to sell seconds, and your lower priced items.

Sample Sales

A sample sale is an organized event where designers sell off samples, seconds, and last season's merchandise. They are like street fairs, in the sense that you have full customer interaction. The audience often consists of a specific targeted market and customer. This is why it is so important to know who your customer is. You could have the best million dollar product idea, but if you hit the wrong market for the sample sale you'll end up wasting your time and money. Attendees usually pay an entrance fee, so they are there specifically to shop. Sample sale participation can range from $50-$2,000. Some well known sample events are Shecky's, Million Dollar Babes, and Thread. Sometimes these events are called trunk shows, but that is not the true definition of a sale like this.

Trunk Shows

The name "trunk show" comes from the past. Designers used to take a trunk of designs to a clothing store and sell directly to the customers. A trunk show these days can describe either a direct or indirect sale. Direct sales are when a boutique offers a designer to come and sell merchandise at their business as a promotion, with the store taking a small percentage. If you are at the store doing the actual selling, the store should not take more than 30% of your sale, because you are the sales person. Trunk shows can be a nice opportunity to expand your client base. You get a captive audience in the store's clientele, and

Notes:

Notes:

the store may also end up carrying your designs if they appeal to their customers.

Home Parties

Oddly enough, this seems to have become the newest rage in selling. The idea is the same as with a Tupperware party or a Pleasure party.

Did you know?

Tupperware parties started as one of the first direct marketing programs in 1946, with housewives getting together to buy and sell the latest Tupperware products. Pleasure parties (also referred to as candle parties) are newer and started in the late 1970s as a way to sell intimate toys and accessories to women, sparing them the embarrassment of going into a store.

More recently, home parties have emerged as a way to sell products that are not available in stores or online. This is a great concept and has gotten more recognition by the media recently. One of the more recognizable names that have taken this route is *Carol Anderson by Invitation* (CABI for short).

With home sales, designers usually seek out reps who sell their line out of their own homes to friends and family, and they take a percentage. Usually, the designer requires the rep to purchase a sample kit at wholesale price; the rep then takes orders, collects the money, and the designer ships directly to the customer or to the rep for distribution.

Retail Store

At first glance, opening your own retail store sounds like a great idea. You can control the way your designs are displayed, you receive direct customer feedback, and you get 100% of the profit. Sounds good, but do you know what it takes to run a store? A store is a full time job, and unless you plan on hiring a full time employee to manage everything, you can easily lose your focus and cause your design work to suffer.

"If you build it, they will come," is a common misconception. That only happens in the movies; like Kevin Costner in "Field of Dreams." To make your sales, you need to get traffic to your store. If you happen to score a prime location in an area with lots of retail shoppers (and can afford the lease), then you have nailed the traffic situation, but what about your time? If you will be in the front of the store selling your merchandise, then what has become of your design business? These are all questions you need to ask yourself before you get much further with the retail idea.

Operating a retail store could be another book entirely, but for now, know that it is not as glamorous as it looks, and the profit isn't as much as you think either. There is a reason why the markup from wholesale to retail is so much. It costs that much to run a shop. From the labor to the fixtures to the million unexpected expenses, it adds up fast.

Once your business is going steady, then you may want to consider opening a store, but running your clothing line is usually a full time job in its own.

Notes:

Notes:

Mail Order

Mail order business is dying down with the rise of internet sales. You may have noticed that you are receiving only one Victoria Secret catalog a month instead of the usual four. Even the Ikea catalogs aren't being sent out as often anymore. It's costly to print catalogs, not to mention targeting your mailing list to those likely to order. By contrast, email marketing campaigns are easy and inexpensive, and they receive the same response, if not more.

Chapter 27
Indirect Sales

Indirect sales are sales that others control. When you sell your product wholesale, you no longer have control over how your merchandise is presented or sold. Although direct sales might seem to be the better option at first, wholesale or indirect sales should be your goal. Wholesale is beneficial to you in that you take orders, produce what is ordered, deliver to your retailers and receive your payment when you deliver. You don't have to wait for the customer to make the purchase before you get paid.

Things may not always go as planned. Retailers may cancel or go out of business before your delivery date, but that is something that will happen. Turn those canceled orders into direct sales. There are several ways to acquire wholesale accounts and here are some brief explanations of them.

Trade Shows

There are two major trade show seasons. The first one is in January/February and features Fall collections; the second is in August/September and features Holiday and Spring collections. There are other trade shows throughout the year, but these are the two main times buyers travel for shows.

Notes:

MAGIC Marketplace
www.magiconline.com

The best known trade shows are the ones held in Las Vegas known as MAGIC Marketplace. Listings of trade shows can be found on Infomat.com.

Ginormous:
gigantic and enormous

MAGIC is <u>ginormous</u> and houses over 20,000 product lines. 80% of the exhibitors are large name designers and typically do not exhibit at other venues. Some of the larger exhibitors have show budget upwards of $50,000 for their exhibits. Independent designers do not have that budget and can easily get lost in the shuffle at a show of this magnitude.

Project
www.projectshow.com

Pool
www.pooltradeshow.com

It's a good idea to walk any show prior to signing up for it to find out if your product fits into the targeted market. The last thing you want to do is invest $10,000 in a show that turns out to be the wrong show for you. During MAGIC, several smaller boutique shows take place, such as Pool and Project, so check those out as well.

Notes:

Ten thousand dollars for participation is not an exaggerated figure. The cost can be upwards of $5,000 for a small booth, and large companies may pay up to 20 grand for the large display spaces. Some of the smaller shows may cost slightly less, but a cost of around $3,000 you can pretty much count on.

Those are just your space fees; you also need to consider your display, transportation to the show, food, and lodging. Most tradeshows will also not let you load up your booth through the front door. You will probably have to arrange for delivery to the show and there is a charge per piece for load in. Fixtures (racks and shelving) may not be included in the space rental. The show organizers may offer these at an additional charge, or you may wish to provide your own.

Preparing for the shows can also be costly. Printed material, website updates, and samples all have to be made ready. You'll also need someone to help run the business while you are out of town for the show, and possibly help with all the follow up calls after you come back.

While this sounds overwhelming, it's not unrealistic for you to consider being in a show. Take two seasons to walk the shows. Fall shows are different than Spring shows. Shows usually last about three days, so my advice is to take the first two days to see what is there, and the last day to talk to the vendors. The last day is usually quiet and the vendors are naturally exhausted. Ask them how they did. Some may share, some won't, but it doesn't hurt to try and get as much info as you can.

Talk to some first time vendors and some seasoned ones. You can probably tell right away who is a first-timer and who is seasoned. You will hear a difference in their sales figures. Most first timers don't sell as much as the ones who have braved it a few times. This is due to their lack of selling experience in a tradeshow environment, as well as to buyers being cautious.

Buyers are hesitant to buy from a new vendor without a history. Once buyers get used to seeing a vendor more then once, they'll feel more confident and may purchase a new line. A continuing presence shows that the designer will be around for more than one season. Buyers of retail establishments cater to their customers and usually have a loyal following. The last thing a buyer wants to do is find an outstanding line or product, have the customer love it, want more, and find out the next season that the designer has gone out of business.

Notes:

Notes:

You've walked your shows, decided which ones work, now its time to commit. Many shows have half booths for first time vendors, so ask about them—they are not always published. But be wary of the booth's locations. Just because something is a good deal pricewise, doesn't mean you should jump on it. It may be priced low for a reason. If the smaller booths are in the last row or back row, you might want to politely decline. People tend to be too tired to walk that last row.

If you have an opportunity to be in the first booth in a row towards the front, chances are, you will get enough sales to cover the cost of a full size booth. Get your best sales person (whether a friend, family member, employee or customer) to help you out. You need to give a great first impression, and the enthusiasm of someone who loves your product will help you sell more.

Last bit of advice. FOLLOW UP. No kidding here. Many vendors do not follow up with people who visit their booths – you can chalk these in the column of lost sales. Take business cards from everyone so you remember who to follow up with. And remember that it's not only buyers who visit your booth; media and the press walk these shows too.

Showrooms

The ultimate hope of any designer at a trade show is to get a showroom. Sales reps often attend the trade shows to find the next biggest brand for their showrooms. Many showrooms won't take you until you've reached a certain number of stores that already carry your collection. Showroom space is high staked real estate. Some showrooms may charge you a monthly rack (or space) fee and then a percentage of sales. Showroom cuts can be 10-25%, plus the monthly fee. The fees and commissions will vary, and there are many items that can be negotiated in your contract with the showroom.

Road Reps

Road Reps are basically traveling salesmen. Road reps work a specific region and have a regular route of boutiques with which they have set up accounts. These reps will take samples to the stores for orders. Road reps often charge a higher commission (25-35%) to account for their travel expenses.

Reps and showrooms will both have contracts for you to sign. Look over the contract and negotiate the terms of payment, exclusivity, percentages, and length of the contract with each account you acquire. Don't just sign on the dotted line.

If you are working with a new rep on the scene, you need to make sure you are covered for possible loss of your samples, so I suggest you take a credit card deposit for your samples until they are returned. Use your best judgment in requesting this information. If you ask this of a showroom that has been around for 10 or more years, you may be laughed at; research and be sure to check up on any references. This will help you establish a relationship of trust without appearing too difficult.

Boutiques

Another way to nail a wholesale account is to be your own rep and contact the boutiques directly. In order to do this successfully, you need to approach or solicit the stores before they head off to market and use their entire buying budget. Approaching stores requires some tact. Store owners and buyers are very busy. It's not appropriate to just walk in and start pitching your line. One way is to call in advance, ask for the

Notes:

Notes:

name and email address of the buyer, and email her information on you line; then follow up with a phone call a week later.

However, the approach I recommend is to visit the local boutiques personally, see if your product will work there, then ask for the card and name of the buyer so you can contact her at a later date. Because buyers are busy bees, disrupting their schedule can be frustrating to them and can possibly leave a bad first impression.

One advantage of selling directly to a boutique is that it creates a personal connection, one which the store owner can carry into selling your product.

Consignment Boutiques

Another well known option is consignment. While many seasoned designers shudder at the word, for a newcomer, this could be your best first step. Consignment is an arrangement where a store agrees to carry a product without purchasing it up front, and pays the designer only after sales are made, usually on a monthly basis. Many small boutiques will offer a new line the consignment option. It presents little risk to the store owner and gives a new designer an insight into what customers are looking for and whether the designer has targeted the correct market.

If you choose to do consignment, make sure you have a signed agreement with the store and a payment schedule. Consignment rates can vary from 40%-80% depending on the boutique. Make sure you find out what the percentage is before setting your price. It is also very important to rotate your merchandise regularly. Many shoppers return monthly to boutiques to see what is new, so keeping merchandise in a boutique on consignment for more than 60 days can cause your clothes to go "stale." Boutiques will usually keep merchandise for longer than 60 days, but at that time, they are usually marked down to make room for new arrivals. If you keep your merchandise fresh and new all the time, your products have a better chance of selling.

When entering into a consignment arrangement, find out who else has worked on consignment with the store and talk to them. Unfortunately, some boutiques don't pay up, and others may close unexpectedly and keep your merchandise. There will always be a risk in consignment. You are going into business on the honor system.

Hot Tip!

Have you considered joining a co-op boutique? These types of boutiques have been around for years and each one is structured slightly differently. Some co-ops charge you rent for rack space only, while others ask you to share in the rent and responsibilities. With this type of arrangement you get direct feedback on your product and a higher percentage of your sales.

Department Stores

You may score a department store order, but be wary. There are hidden costs and requirements that department stores follow which can really be unsavory for an independent designer. All large stores require bar-coding of your product. Barcodes can be purchased individually or you can purchase the system that

Notes:

Notes:

generates them. Individual barcodes run about $25 each. Even after you get your barcode, the stores require merchandise to be packaged a certain way, in plastic wrap and on hangers. They are also very picky about delivery dates. If they do not receive a product on a specific date, they may refuse your shipment and you can be left with a whole lot of inventory on your hands.

Once you jump all the hoops and get into a department store, there is yet another trap to watch for. Payment dates. Some may pay up to 120 days after receipt. That's four months of no income. And of course there is the chargeback.

Chargebacks:
charges to the design company when discounts are given by the retailer. A practice used by department stores. This can also be referred to as Markdown Money.

Chargebacks are a nasty surprise to newbies in the business, so you should know a little on how they work. Let's say you sell 1,000 items at the wholesale price of $10 each to Macy's and they marked the garment up to $40 retail. 30 days later they mark down the garment to $30. Macy's is still making a profit of $20, but that $10 they marked down they now consider a loss and they make you responsible for half of that markdown, which is $5 (half your wholesale price). 60 days go by and they mark the merchandise down to $10 to move it. The markdown is $30, and you are still responsible for half of it or $15. You could now owe money to the department store for the merchandise you sold to them!

Notes:

There is no way around chargebacks, but there are ways you can protect your profits from being eaten by a department store. If a department store expresses an interest in your line, limit their orders and don't put all your eggs in their basket. Diversify your sales channels. Make sure you target smaller boutiques where there is no chance of a chargeback. Consider your merchandise in a department store as part of your advertising budget. It's great exposure to sell in a department store, but decide how much you would spend on advertising and limit their orders to that expected expense.

Payment terms

Whoever you end up working with—a rep, a showroom, or a store—you need to be clear on your payment terms. If you are upfront with your accounts, there should not be an issue with this. You should require COD or credit card payment until you have a steady cash flow or you establish a relationship with a store. You can explain to the stores and reps that you are a small business and can't wait 30 days for payment. Once you have the product and you are ready to ship, call the stores to let them know it is being shipped and their credit card is being charged.

Collecting Debt

What do you do if a store - for example one where you have merchandise on consignment—doesn't pay up?

I personally had a consignment arrangement with a boutique that went AWOL without paying. When I went to switch inventory I discovered that the store had closed, and my inventory had gone with it. I later found out they liquidated their entire inventory on eBay, kept the cash, and ran. Did I ever collect? No.

How do you avoid getting into this situation? You can't avoid the risk entirely, but you can take steps to reduce it. Check up on your inventory every two to four weeks. Stop by the store and rotate your inventory regularly. Do your homework - get to know the stores and compare notes with other designers who

Notes:

Net 30—payment is due 30 days from the date of the invoice

might have consignment agreements with those boutiques. You last option is to take the store into Collections or to Small Claims Court. There are agencies that will facilitate collections for you in exchange for a percentage of the amount they collect for you. This can be done for consignment boutiques as well as for stores where you have an arrangement of Net 30 or more.

Chapter 28
Line Sheets

Lines sheets are a way of organizing your collection for a prospective buyer. Line sheets contain flat images and sometimes photos of the pieces in your collection. Line sheets give information about the company, buying options, minimums, prices, fabric details, colors, size charts, and care instructions.

Keep a copy of your line sheets in a PDF format so it can be emailed to prospective buyers. If you wish to add a link on your website to your line sheet, you may want to password protect it, so only retail buyers can have access to it.

Following are two examples of types of line sheets. The first is typical of a traditional line sheet with flats and product details. This example defines the season, the date range for delivery and pricing (both wholesale and retail).

The second example is a blend of a line sheet and a look book (which I provide more details in the following chapter). This appears more as a catalog, but serves the same purpose and is just as effective.

Notes:

Example

Loyale Clothing, www.loyaleclothing.com

loyale

spring/summer 2007 – delivery: march 15 - april 1
close date: november 1

FABRIC: hemp / organic cotton linen COLOR: navy mustard coral bone SIZING: xs – l	FABRIC: hemp / organic cotton linen COLOR: navy mustard SIZING: xs – l
wholesale price: $ 84 suggested retail: $ 168 madera dress sp07 d112	wholesale price: $ 92 suggested retail: $ 184 pasadena dress sp07 d108
FABRIC: 100% bamboo jersey COLOR: navy mustard teal coral bone SIZING: xs – l	FABRIC: 100% bamboo jersey COLOR: navy mustard teal coral bone SIZING: xs – l
wholesale price: $ 30 suggested retail: $ 60 calexico top sp07 t113	wholesale price: $ 26 suggested retail: $ 52 escondido slip sp07 d114
FABRIC: 100% bamboo jersey COLOR: navy mustard teal coral bone SIZING: xs – l	FABRIC: hemp / organic cotton linen COLOR: navy mustard teal coral bone SIZING: xs – l
wholesale price: $ 74 suggested retail: $ 148 sonora dress sp07 d115	wholesale price: $ 78 suggested retail: $ 156 vista dress sp07 d113

Example

Buhl Company Inc., www.buhlzone.com

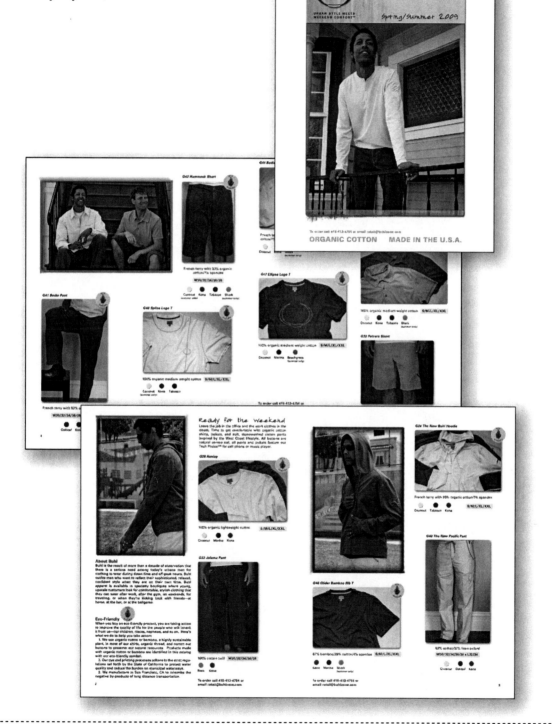

Chapter 29
Look books

Look books are mini catalogues of your collection. Some look books carry detailed information that can be found on a line sheet such as the last example, these are photographic representations of your work and are produced at a high quality.

Look books are not as financially feasible as a line sheet would be and can be wasteful if they are not distributed in a timely manner. The price for printing is not inexpensive. Not only are you fronting the cost of the actual look book, but you are also responsible for the composure of the book. Booking the models, photography, hair and makeup and the layout of the book are not likely to be free.

Look books are usually distributed at tradeshows or by direct mail. My advice is to seriously consider the cost in preparing a look book over a line sheet. Both options can be equally effective and one of them will save you $$.

Notes:

Example

M the Movement, www.mthemovement.com

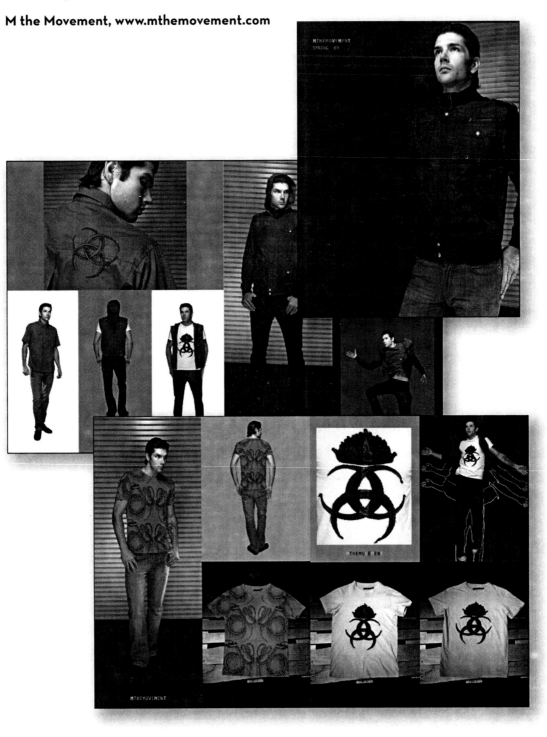

STARTING YOUR BUSINESS

Chapter 30
Business Entity

In simpler times, all you had to do to go into business was hang a shingle over your door. Today, to do it properly, you have to set up your business legally. Where do you start? I will guide you through the basic process, but I highly recommend you check with your local government offices for registration and permit guidelines.

Many local governments have web pages set up specifically for small businesses. The Small Business Administration (SBA) website also has general guides on setting up your business, as well as links to free or inexpensive workshops and seminars.

Sole Proprietorship

A sole proprietorship is the easiest to set up, mainly because you don't have to do anything different from what you're probably already doing. You continue to file your taxes on your personal Form 1040, with the addition of a Schedule C. If you have ever worked as a contractor, you should be familiar with Schedule C because you've used it to write off your business expenses.

Although this is a simple way of doing business, it can get complicated really fast. If you default on any business debts,

Notes:

Small Business Administration:
SBA.gov

Notes:

you can be held personally liable and your personal property can be at risk. Besides personal liability, it may also be harder to seek funding under this operation.

General Partnerships

A general partnership results automatically when 2 or more people go into business together. Most partners in a business sign a partnership agreement defining the general terms of their business relationship. With general partnerships, both profits and liabilities are split between the partners according to the agreement.

Needless to say, know the person you are about to become business partners with. Personal differences and misunderstandings can easily cause aggravation and even bring a business down. If one partner makes improper decisions for the business, the other may end up on the hook for them.

Joint Ventures

A joint venture acts as a general partnership with the exception that it is set up for a limited period of time or for a particular project.

Limited Liability Company & Limited Liability Partnership

A Limited Liability Company (LLC) and Limited Liability Partnerships (LLP) are legal setups designed to offer liability protection of personal assets in case things start to go wrong with your business. You can form an LLC whether you are sole owner or in a partnership. An LLP is a route many general partnerships opt for. An LLC or LLP is best set up with the assistance of a lawyer. Although both LLCs and LLPs are designed to protect you and your partners from business mistakes, there are important exceptions. Do your research and make sure the advantages of this business setup will work for you before jumping into it.

C-Corporations & S-Corporations

A corporation is comprised of shareholders or stockholders. This type of company is a unique entity and is taxed as such. Set up is complicated and costly to maintain and there are stringent record-keeping requirements. An S-Corporation is a version of the regular, or C-Corporation, with a different tax filing. Consult with a lawyer before deciding on this type of entity.

Many independent designers originally start out as sole proprietorships. As their business grows, their needs may change and a different business entity may become necessary. A tax or business lawyer may be able to advise you on what's the best set up for each stage of your business.

There are many services online that advertise legal setups at affordable prices. Be wary, as these services typically offer forms that are generic and may not protect you. A lawyer will cost you a little extra up front but you'll know the job has been done right. If you do decide to use a do-it-yourself legal company, check them out with the Better Business Bureau to make sure you are dealing with an upright company. Nolo.com has excellent resources and products to help you legally set up your business.

Keep in mind that you can always change your business entity down the road. You might be just fine developing your product as a sole proprietor, then change your entity when your business is actually producing revenue. Consult with your lawyer before making your decision.

Notes:

Better Business Bureau:
www.BBB.org

Business entity forms and resources:
www.Nolo.com

Chapter 31
Licenses and Permits

Fictitious Business Name

You will need to file a Fictitious Business Name Statement if you plan on operating your business with a name other than your own legal name. This name statement is filed with your city or county government. Make sure to conduct a search for the name you are planning on using before actually filing it. You may be surprised to discover that a catering company or a dry cleaner has already registered that name. These searches are usually available online and can be found on your city or county government website.

There is a minimal registration fee for this, and you are required to post the fictitious name in a local paper. Many papers specialize in this type of posting. Your mailbox will be flooded with offers on where you can have it posted, so don't worry about planning out which paper to post it in advance.

Business License and Taxes

You will also have to file for a business license with the city you are operating your business in. You will need your Fictitious Business Name Statement in order to do this. You may also need to file for zoning permits. The zoning permits regulate the type of business

Notes:

Notes:

allowable in your area. If you are operating out of your home, your business may have to be designated a home occupation or hobby. Your city government can point you in the right direction.

The business license is usually not a large investment. You may have to pay for any zoning permits that go with the license. Your business license is reviewed annually, and to do that, you must file your business taxes with your city each year. Forms will be mailed automatically to you, so make sure to let your city business office know if you are moving.

Sellers Permit

You are required you to have a Sellers Permit/Resale Number through the State Board of Equalization if you sell merchandise. This is sometimes called a "Use Tax." There is a nominal fee, and the permit allows you to purchase your fabrics, notions, and other goods at wholesale prices without being charged sales tax. It also requires you to collect sales tax on goods sold directly to the public. If you sell directly to a retailer with the intent of your goods being resold, you do not need to collect sales tax; it becomes the retailer's responsibility to collect it. You will be required to file your Use Tax Return with the state either annually, quarterly, or monthly, depending on what you chose when you filed for your number.

Employer's Identification Number

EIN Filing:
http://www.irs.gov/
businesses/small/
article/0,,id=98350,00.
html

If you are operating your business as a sole proprietorship, you may use your Social Security number for your business, or you may file for an Employer's Identification Number (EIN) from the IRS, using Form SS-4. Forms are available online at IRS.gov, and filing is free. All other business entities must operate under an EIN.

Chapter 32
Financial Basics

Business Bank Accounts

You'll need to get a business checking account as soon as you have filed for your business license and fictitious business name. You will need these documents in order to set up your accounts. Once you set up a business checking account, apply for a business credit card. To keep things orderly, use your business credit card only for business purchases and personal credit cards for personal purchases. You might want to apply for a business credit card at the same time you set up your checking account. You can sometimes link the two together for overdraft protection and you can only do that if they are with the same bank.

Taxes

Set reminders on your calendar. Put post-its on your door. Write yourself notes on your mirror with lipstick. Do whatever it takes, but remember to file your taxes. If you don't, those wonderful people at the IRS can come knocking on your door asking to audit you. You will be fined if you do not file your taxes in a timely manner.

Notes:

Notes:

Remember these dates:

- Your business taxes need to be filed annually.
- Use taxes need to be filed annually, quarterly or monthly.
- Business property taxes are annual.
- Unemployment Taxes (if you have employees) are filed monthly.
- Income tax filing date is April 15th.

If you collect sales tax from customers, set this money aside and keep an accurate record of what you owe to the state. Do not commingle it with other accounts or make the mistake of spending it on some urgent expense. Not paying all of your sales tax when it comes due can get you some stiff penalties.

Hot Tip!

You may want to open a savings account for your sales tax. This way, you get to collect interest on government money. Maybe the interest earned will treat you to a new pair of shoes or a massage.

Insurance

Not having insurance is like playing Russian roulette with your business. Seek out and invest in business insurance that is appropriate for your business. You may need liability insurance in case somebody gets injured on your property. Liability insurance can also cover you on lawsuits against your business. Ask your insurance agent about coverage of your inventory and business property, and coverage for theft and loss of business. There are many levels of insurance coverage, costing from

$50 a month to $300 a month or more. You may also want to consider product liability coverage. This coverage protects you against faulty products and product injury.

If you have employees, you are required by law to have workers compensation insurance. Workers Comp covers employees if they injure themselves on the job or become disabled.

Notes:

Chapter 33
Funding Your Business

Bootstrapping

Bootstrapping is not exactly funding, but it's what most of us do when first settling on the idea of working for ourselves. Basically, you hold a job, freelance, or take on a position part-time to fund your company. If this is how you plan to do it, it's important that you maintain a strict budget and only set a certain amount of funds aside for your business. Spend only what you budget.

Website to Check Out:
entrepreneur.com

Start-up Capital

You have saved up by scrimping and working nights and weekends. This is part of your start-up capital, but you may need to raise more. The start-up capital can come from all kinds of sources. Savings accounts, investment accounts (401(k) & retirement accounts), selling a car or other assets, borrowing against a house, borrowing from friends and family, and credit cards can all be used to fund your start-up or as collateral for a business loan. If you can avoid tapping into the last resource (credit cards), please do so. Using or maxing out your credit

Notes:

_____

_____

_____

_____

_____

_____

_____

_____

cards can not only be detrimental to your credit score but will cause banks to turn down loan applications. Friends and family may be your best bet, but be careful to make arrangements for returning the payment. You can use social lending companies to set up friends and family lending. This will assure them that you will pay them back.

Micro-Loans

The Small Business Association works with several banks in assisting small businesses with loans they may not otherwise qualify for. An SBA-guaranteed bank loan is called a micro-loan. The interest rate on these types of loans is usually higher than traditional bank-term loans, but they are easier to obtain. These loans are ideal for startups though existing companies use them too. You will need to have money in the bank in order to qualify for the loan; this is where the start-up capital comes in. You will need to show the bank how much you have already invested or how much you are willing to invest, show them a business plan with your projections, and offer up any collateral available. These loans range from a couple hundred dollars up to $20,000.

Bank-Term Loans

Bank-term loans are usually for established businesses and are typically used to expand a business. These loans start around $25,000. They are not usually an option for independent designers, but don't rule it out. Talk to your bank about what conditions you must satisfy to qualify.

Virtual Bank Loans

Virtual banks live all over the internet. Interest may be lower than micro-loans and easier to obtain than bank-term loans.

Be careful before signing up for one though, as not everyone on the internet is a legitimate lender. Your local community development offices may have recommendations on virtual bank loans or loan programs that you may qualify for.

Social Lending Sources

Social or peer-to-peer lending is the newest form of lending and is quite different from traditional loans. Applicants get qualified based on their loan application as well as their individual story. Social lending serves two purposes. It allows anyone who chooses to lend, to do so. It also helps many people obtain a loan, who may not otherwise be qualified to get a loan from a bank. There are presently three social lending websites participating in this type of lending, but more will follow the lead as the popularity of this type of peer-to-peer lending grows.

Social Lending Websites: prosper.com, lendingclub. com, zopa.com

The three companies that currently assist with social lending are Prosper, Zopa and Lending Club.

- Prosper – Peer-to-peer lending where each individual makes the ultimate decision on who gets the loans.

- Lending Club – Much like Prosper, but is not available in every state.

- Zopa – Based in the UK; your credit score is the ultimate factor determining whether you'll get a loan.

There are advantages and disadvantages to social lending. Advantages: As a borrower, you may qualify for a loan even if you don't when screened by a traditional institution. As a lender, you can invest in other peoples and build an investment plan to suit your needs.

Notes:

Notes:

....

....

....

....

....

....

....

....

....

....

....

....

....

....

Factoring services:
apparelsearch.com/
factors.htm

Articles on Factoring:
businessfinancemag.com/
print/6442 and guideye.
com/story/factoring_in_
the_fashion_business_
better_than_going_to_
the_bank

Disadvantages: As a borrower, your interest rates may be higher than with bank loans if your credit score is blemished. As a lender, you may be at risk if borrowers default on their loans.

Venture Capital

Venture capital is usually provided by professionally managed firms that loan large amount to high growth companies capable of reaching $25 million in sales by the 5th year. Venture capitalists (VCs) expect equity ownership in exchange for the investment. This is not really a practical option for independent designers.

Angel Investors

An angel investor is very similar to a VC, but is an individual rather than a company. Angel investors expect ownership percentage and sometimes require involvement in the business to help create a return on their investment.

Factoring

Factoring is having a loan secured by orders taken. Factoring may not be an option for you if you have less than lustrous credit or have not built up your business credit. Factors are lenders who lend money based on the total amount of orders placed with your company.

The loan typically does not cover the entire amount of your orders. Payment is due as soon as orders are shipped and money is collected. If you have cancellations, you are still responsible for immediate payment. Not all factors will lend on all orders, especially small design firms that don't have business credit. The businesses placing the orders must also have sound credit in order for a factor to cover your orders.

Knowing your Personal Credit

When embarking onto your own business venture, you really need to be aware of your credit and the information that the credit bureaus have. Make sure to obtain your credit report prior to applying for any loan and go over it carefully. You do not want to discover a surprise item on your credit report after you've applied for a loan. Credit scores range from 300 to 850. Any score under a 680 can cause lenders to be less than forthcoming with their money. Once you check your credit, I suggest you keep an eye on it. Credit monitoring services can help in this matter and alert you when new activity appears on your credit file.

However, they may not always alert you in a timely manner when new activity shows up under your name. It can take months for you to learn that a new account has been opened in your name, and that may have been enough time to cause damage. I suggest you get a copy of your credit report regularly (once a year is free), so you can be sure it reflects your profile accurately for future business. Check on all your past credit as well. Are there accounts that are showing open even though you closed them 10 years ago? This can adversely affect your overall credit score. Call or write to the parties involved, request that they fix the error, and keep on them until they do.

What if you discover that your identity was stolen and the thief has run up credit on your name? Contact the company that issued the credit immediately, explain your problem, and stay with it until it gets resolved. This happens more frequently than you might think and can happen in all kinds of ways. When running a business, you will be particularly vulnerable as you will be using your credit cards, bank

Guidance on Reviewing and Fixing Credit: Credit.com

Notes:

Notes:

cards, and checks a lot more than before. Each use gives an opportunity for theft.

Here are a few suggestions on how to keep your information safe.

- Purchases online should be done with a credit card and not a bank/debit card. If your bank account is hit, you will feel it immediately and it may take time to get that money back. On the other hand, with credit cards, you're generally not responsible for fraudulent charges, and will not feel a financial impact while things are straightened out.
- Use certain cards for certain things. Try not to mix up your business card with your personal card.
- Sign up for online banking and check your bank account balances often. Make sure your computer has virus protection.
- Do not send financial information or passwords over email or by cell phone. Emails can be easily hacked and cell phone calls can be intercepted.

Credit for your Business

So far I've discussed protecting your personal credit, but what you may be interested in is building your business credit. Business credit scores range from 0–100. 75 and up is considered to be excellent. Dun & Bradstreet provide business credit scores, as well as a handful of other companies. Business credit profiles usually cost a few hundred dollars to set up. Good business credit is important if you plan on working with factors or if you plan on establishing credit terms with suppliers and contractors.

Dun & Bradstreet
Business Credit Scores:
smallbusiness.dnb.com

Chapter 34
Protecting Your Work

Most designers' biggest fear is having their designs stolen, and there is a good reason for it. If you pay attention to fashion, you see similarities among clothing lines all the time—from colors to fabrics and designs. The first thing you need to accept is that in fashion there is nothing ever really 100% original. As designers, we pull inspiration from the past, the present, and yes, other designers.

To tell someone that you have never pulled inspiration from another person's clothing is foolish. Artists are inspired by everything, and unless you are blind, you cannot make that statement without holding your fingers crossed. Having said this, where do we draw the line between inspiration and stealing?

Traditionally, "knocking off" a design happened after the design was released out into the world, so it was known who the designer was that originated it. Although, did that designer really originate it?

Notes:

Notes:

Big names aren't exempt from "knocking off" designs. Despite all their fame, brand name designers have been caught for stealing. Yves Saint Laurent took Ralph Lauren to court in 1994 for stealing a tuxedo dress design and won in a French court.

Design theft happens on all sides of the trade. For smaller designers, it's a particular concern. How and where can this happen to a smaller designer? Trade shows for one. Many larger companies hire their designers to walk the trade shows, find designs that are fabulous, and knock them off or be "inspired" by them. All the big names do it. Maybe it was coincidence, but did that blouse really mean to have the exact same pattern mistake in the neckline?

The second most common way to steal is in the actual production of the garments. The danger lies usually in overseas production, primarily out of Chinese factories. Because the factory controls how and when your product is finished, if they decide to knock off your design, they can get it on the shelf before yours and at a lesser price. This can seriously hurt a designer. To ease your fears, I suggest having any international manufacturer sign an exclusivity agreement to limit their production of your garments to you. Not everyone will do it, but if they say no, think twice about using their services.

Are you scared yet? Are you tossing and turning at night, wondering how to avoid the threat of imminent piracy? You should always be designing new and original pieces for your collection. If you launch your business betting on one design only, what happens to your company if you get knocked off? You'll be out of business in a jiffy.

The best things you can do to protect yourself against the loss of business is to build your brand loyalty. If you have a targeted audience and they love you and your designs, who cares if H & M steals from you. Look at it as flattery – a big name thinks your designs are worth stealing. Get the word out in your social media networks. This type of news travels faster than TV anyway. Make sure you can back up your claims.

You also have some legal means of protecting your designs, but not as good as you might wish. If you live in Europe, you are in better luck. There are copyright laws there that protect your designs longer than the life of the actual garment. If you live in the US, sorry guys, no such protection yet, although there are some acts in the works. But even if these laws are passed, how will they be enforced? Will there be a large influx of lawsuits? And against who? The small designer who can't afford a lawyer or the big guys?

Copyrights vs. Design Piracy Prohibition Act (HR 2033)

The Design Piracy Prohibition Act is a proposed legislation to enhance protection of fashion designs by changing copyright law. A copyright currently protects works of authorship, such as writings, music, and works of art that have been tangibly expressed. The Library of Congress registers copyrights which last for the life of the author plus 70 years. In more recent years, the law has been changed to accommodate design of ship hulls, but limits it to 10 years. Copyrights currently do not protect "useful items," which pertains to clothing.

The proposed act would include protection for fashion designs in copyright law, but for three years only. Europe has laws similar to the U.S.'s proposed legislation, and protects their registered fashion designs for 25 years. The U.S. has had the act

Notes:

Informational Article:
Protecting works of fashion from design piracy by Christine Magno. http://leda. law.harvard.edu/leda/ data/36/magdo.html

**Read about Fashion Piracy:** BPCouncil.com, stopfashionpiracy.com

Notes:

presented twice in the past few years, neither time making its way fully through congress. The first legislation was presented in 2006 as HR 5055 and again in 2007 as HR 2033. Even though it appears to be stagnant in congress, I'm sure this is not the last we will hear of it, so I will explain a little more about what the law would protect if it passes.

To understand what the Design Piracy Prohibition Act actually protects, it's probably best to discuss what it doesn't protect. It doesn't protect items that are "useful" that have been in the market place more than three months prior to registering the design. In other words, if you don't claim protection at the time you release your design, you are out of luck.

Ultimately, the law would protect the designers who have the money to register their designs and to seek lawsuits against copycats. It's most useful aspect however is that it will put a stop to the counterfeiting that goes on overseas, and the importing of those counterfeits. No more fake LV bags in the alleys of Chinatown. The act will penalize the companies that buy the counterfeits and restrict sales in the U.S.

Tip from an insider at Banana Republic:

If a big name company steals your design, get yourself some legal council. They will fold at the sound of a lawsuit or bad press.

Trademarks

Trademarks can't protect your design, but they can protect your trade name or your logo. A trademark is a type of intellectual property, typically a name, word, phrase, logo, symbol, design, image, or a combination of these elements. Trademarks protect words, names, symbols, sounds, or colors that distinguish goods and services from those manufactured or sold by others and indicate the source of the goods. Trademarks, unlike patents, can be renewed forever as long as they are being used in commerce. Trademarks cost between $275 and $325 to register in the U.S., depending on the classification. You can also register trademarks in other countries if you plan on working internationally.

Patents

A patent also will not protect a clothing design, but will protect functionality in the design. If you have developed a new way to use a current product, you may be able to have it patented. If you wish to proceed with a patent, you must have deep pockets and a lawyer who enjoys filling theirs. For smaller designers, patents aren't really an option unless you really have created something new and plan on investing $20,000 to protect it. It costs $540 to file at the U.S. Patent Office, then about $19,460 for the lawyer to follow up on it ($540 + $19,460 = $20,000 investment).

Confidentiality Agreement and Non Disclosure Agreements

Your best bet, if you're worried about your designs, is to have any contractors you are dealing with sign a Confidentiality Agreement or a Non-Disclosure Agreement. This is customary and protects you from having your contractor sell your secrets to your competitors or share your patterns with them.

The following agreement is an example of one I use professionally in commerce when working with freelance consultants.

Notes:

CONFIDENTIAL INFORMATION AND NONDISCLOSURE AGREEMENT

As a condition of my becoming retained as a consultant (or my consulting relationship being continued) by Jennifer Lynne Matthews and Porcelynne Lingerie organized under the laws of the state of California, (the "Company"), and in consideration of my consulting relationship with the Company and my receipt of the compensation now and hereafter paid to me by the Company, I agree to the following:

1. **Consulting Relationship.** I understand and acknowledge that this Confidential Information and Nondisclosure Agreement (the "Agreement") does not alter, amend or expand upon any rights I may have to continue in a consulting relationship with, or in the duration of my consulting relationship with, the Company under any existing agreements between the Company and me, or under applicable law. Any consulting relationship between the Company and me, whether commenced prior to or upon the date of this Agreement, shall be referred to herein as the "Relationship."

2. **Confidential Information and Nondisclosure of Company Information.** I agree at all times during the term of my Relationship with Company and thereafter, to hold in strictest confidence, and not to use, except for the benefit of Company to the extent necessary to perform my obligations to the Company under the Relationship, or to disclose to any person, firm, corporation or other entity without written authorization of the Company, any Confidential Information (as defined below) of the Company which I obtain or create. I further agree not to make copies of such Confidential Information except as authorized by the Company. I understand that "Confidential Information" means any Company proprietary information, technical data, trade secrets or know-how, including, but not limited to, research, product plans, products, product names, services, suppliers, contacts, customer lists and customers (including, but not limited to, customers of the Company on whom I called or with whom I became acquainted during the Relationship), prices and costs, markets, software, developments, inventions, notebooks, processes, formulas, technology, patterns, designs, drawings, engineering, hardware configuration information, marketing information, licenses, finances and financial data, budgets, electronic communications, graphic communications, marketing information, proposed trademarks, proposed patents, or other business information disclosed to me by the Company either directly or indirectly in writing, orally or by drawings or observation of parts, products or equipment or created by me during the period of the Relationship, whether or not during working hours. I understand that "Confidential Information" includes, but is not limited to, information pertaining to any aspects of the Company's business which is either information not known by actual or potential competitors of the Company or other third parties not under confidentiality obligations to the Company, or is otherwise proprietary information of the Company or its customers or suppliers, whether of a technical nature or otherwise. I further understand that Confidential Information does not include any of the foregoing items which has become publicly and widely known and made generally available through no wrongful act of mine or of others who were under confidentiality obligations as to the item or items involved.

3. **Inventions Retained and Licensed.** I have attached hereto, as Exhibit A, a list describing with particularity all inventions, original works of authorship, developments, improvements, and trade secrets which were made by me prior to the commencement of the Relationship (collectively referred to as "Prior Inventions"), which belong solely to me or belong to me jointly with another, which relate in any way to any of the Company's proposed businesses or products, and which are not assigned to the Company hereunder; or, if no such list is attached, I represent that there are no such Prior Inventions. If, in the course of my Relationship with the Company, I incorporate into a Company product or process a Prior Invention owned by me or in which I have an interest, the Company is hereby granted and shall have a non-exclusive, royalty-free, irrevocable, perpetual, worldwide license (with the right to sublicense) to make, have made, copy, modify, make derivative works of, use, sell and otherwise distribute such Prior Invention as part of or in connection with such product.

4. **Returning Company Documents.** I agree that, at the time of termination of my Relationship with the Company, I will deliver to the Company (and will not keep in my possession, recreate or deliver to anyone else) any and all Confidential Information and devices, records, data, notes, reports, proposals, lists, correspondence, specifications, drawings, blueprints, sketches, notebooks, materials, flow charts, equipment, other documents or property, or reproductions of any of the aforementioned items, developed by me pursuant to the Relationship or otherwise belonging to the Company, its successors or assigns.

5. **Solicitation of Other Parties.** For a period of twenty-four (24) months following termination of my Relationship with the Company for any reason, with or without cause, I shall not solicit any licensor to or customer of the Company or licensee of the Company's products, in each case, that are known to me, with respect to any business, products or services that are competitive to the products or services offered by the Company or under development as of the date of termination of my Relationship with the Company.

6. **Representations and Covenants.**

This Agreement is for example purposes for this book only and should not in any way be deemed to be legal advice. Each Company should consult with its respective legal counsel to draft an agreement that is appropriate to the Company's specific business purposes and that satisfies all applicable state and other related jurisdictional laws and procedures.

(a) **Facilitation of Agreement.** I agree to execute promptly any proper oath or verify any proper document required to carry out the terms of this Agreement upon the Company's written request to do so.

(b) **Conflicts.** I represent that my performance of all the terms of this Agreement does not and will not breach any agreement I have entered into, or will enter into with any third party, including without limitation any agreement to keep in confidence proprietary information acquired by me in confidence or in trust prior to commencement of my Relationship with the Company. I agree that, in advance of accepting or agreeing to perform consulting services or other services for companies who businesses or proposed businesses in any way involve products or services which would be competitive with the Company's products or services, or those products or services proposed or in development by the Company during the term of the Consulting Agreement, I will promptly notify the Company in writing, specifying the organization with which I propose to consult, become employed by, or otherwise provide services to, and provide information sufficient to allow the Company to determine if such work would conflict with the interests of the Company or further services which the Company might request of me.

(c) **Voluntary Execution.** I certify and acknowledge that I have carefully read all of the provisions of this Agreement and that I understand and will fully and faithfully comply with such provisions.

7. **General Provisions.**

(a) **Governing Law.** The validity, interpretation, construction and performance of this Agreement shall be governed by the laws of the State of California, without giving effect to the principles of conflict of laws.

(b) **Entire Agreement.** This Agreement sets forth the entire agreement and understanding between the Company and me relating to the subject matter herein and merges all prior discussions between us. No modification or amendment to this Agreement, nor any waiver of any rights under this Agreement, will be effective unless in writing signed by both parties.

(c) **Severability.** If any term or provision of this Agreement or the application thereof to any circumstance shall, in any jurisdiction and to any extent, be invalid or unenforceable, such term or provision shall be ineffective as to such jurisdiction to the extent of such invalidity or unenforceability without invalidating or rendering unenforceable the remaining terms and provisions of this Agreement or the application of such terms and provisions to circumstances other than those as to which it is held invalid or unenforceable, and a suitable and equitable term or provision shall be substituted therefor to carry out, insofar as may be valid and enforceable, the intent and purpose of the invalid or unenforceable term or provision. In the event that any court or government agency of competent jurisdiction determines that my provision of services to the Company is not as an independent contractor but instead as an employee under the applicable laws, then solely to the extent that such determination is applicable, references in this Agreement to the Relationship between me and the Company shall be interpreted to include an employment relationship, and this Agreement shall not be invalid and unenforceable but shall be read to the fullest extent as may be valid and enforceable under the applicable laws to carry out the intent and purpose of the Agreement.

(d) **Successors and Assigns.** This Agreement will be binding upon my heirs, executors, administrators and other legal representatives, and my successors and assigns, including, in the event that Consultant is an entity, any successor entity, and will be for the benefit of the Company, its successors, and its assigns.

(e) **Survival.** The provisions of this Agreement shall survive the termination of the Relationship and the assignment of this Agreement by the Company to any successor in interest or other assignee.

(f) **ADVICE OF COUNSEL.** I ACKNOWLEDGE THAT, IN EXECUTING THIS AGREEMENT, I HAVE HAD THE OPPORTUNITY TO SEEK THE ADVICE OF INDEPENDENT LEGAL COUNSEL, AND I HAVE READ AND UNDERSTOOD ALL OF THE TERMS AND PROVISIONS OF THIS AGREEMENT. THIS AGREEMENT SHALL NOT BE CONSTRUED AGAINST ANY PARTY BY REASON OF THE DRAFTING OR PREPARATION HEREOF.

The parties have executed this Agreement on the respective dates set forth below:

COMPANY:

Jennifer Lynne, Porcelynne Lingerie

Signature: _____

Date: _____

CONSULTANT:

an Individual, on behalf of _____

Signature: _____

Date: _____

This Agreement is for example purposes for this book only and should not in any way be deemed to be legal advice. Each Company should consult with its respective legal counsel to draft an agreement that is appropriate to the Company's specific business purposes and that satisfies all applicable state and other related jurisdictional laws and procedures.

LAWS AND REGULATIONS

Chapter 35
Labeling Requirements

Take a look in your closet. Do half of your garments have labels on them that read "Dry Clean Only"? How many of them have you washed, and discovered they do just fine in the laundry? Do you ever wonder—how does this all-knowing manufacturer came up with the care instructions anyway?

Let's answer the "Dry Clean Only" question first. Many companies see this as a get out of jail free card. It's no fault of theirs if you wash your garment and ruin it; they warned you to dry cleaned only. Here is a little about the laws of labeling.

Labeling is regulated by the Federal Trade Commission (FTC), though a series of acts, called the Textile and Wool Acts. The FTC requires every clothing item that is sold in the U.S. to be accompanied by a label stating the fabric content, care instructions, and country of origin. Your registration number (RN) also needs to be on this label.

Notes:

Textile and Wool Acts:
www.ftc.gov/bcp/edu/
pubs/business/textile/
bus21.shtm

RN Filing:
http://www.ftc.gov/bcp/
edu/pubs/consumer/
alert083.shtm

The care instructions on your sewn-in label must include wash instructions (hand or machine), water temperature, type of soap, and drying method, or instructions for dry cleaning. You may ask, "How do I know how to determine the care instruction for my garments?" You should test your garments for shrinkage as well as see the recommendations by your fabric supplier.

Laundry Instructions
and Fabric Care:
Textilecare.com

The Textile and Wool Acts require the fiber content (in percentages) to be either on your sewn-in label or an attached hang tag. The FTC also regulates what fabrics can and cannot be used for specific markets. For example, many fleece fabrics are considered flammable and are not permitted in children's clothing or accessories. Make sure to read the document titled "Threading Your Way Through the Labeling Requirements Under the Textile and Wool Acts" to see if any other restrictions apply to you.

Fabric Education:
Fabriclink.com

What's another reason of important to know the fiber content of a garment? Many people are allergic to fibers originated from animals such as wool or angora. The recently passed Consumer Products Safety Improvement Act strengths these laws. More on this act in Chapter 39.

Chapter 36
State Garment Laws

To deter the persistence of sweatshops, a few states have established labor restrictions for the sewn products industry. The laws are originated by the state's Labor Commissioners and presently exist in California, New York, and New Jersey. Even if you are a business in another state, you may be required to abide by these laws if you do any business with contractors in those states. Contact the state's labor board to find out if you specifically need to register.

Garment Registration of California

California implemented its garment laws in 1978 and last revised them in 1999. The laws require that if your company exists in California, or you do business with a contractor in California, you must register with the labor board. Both contractors and manufacturers must register. As a designer or entrepreneur you are considered a manufacturer by law. This classification exists if you contract work from any individual who cuts, sews, processes, repairs, finishes, or assembles a sewn product. These fees range depending on revenue. Manufacturers' fees start at $750 annually.

To register with the labor board, you must fill out an application, pay the fee determined by your revenue to the

Notes:

CA Registration:
www.dir.ca.gov/dlse/
howtoobtaingarment
registration.htm

To find out whether a factory is registered:
www.dir.ca.gov/ databases/dlselr/ garmreg.html

California Division of Labor Standards (DLSE), and pass a state administered exam regarding labor laws.

Failing to register may result in being charged with a misdemeanor, paying a hefty fine, and having your inventory confiscated. The contractors you use can also be slapped with a fine.

New Jersey Registration

NJ Registration:
www.lwd.dol.state.nj.us/ labor/wagehour/content/ apparel_industry.html

Registration in the state of New Jersey costs $300 annually for manufacturers. Failure to register can bring on a number of charges and penalties. New Jersey laws appear to be the strictest, and they carry the largest penalties. Violations can result in a three year waiting period before being able to begin manufacturing again. Confiscation of inventory, apparel and equipment is a possible penalty.

New York Registration

NY Registration:
www.labor.state.ny.us/ workerprotection/ laborstandards/ workprot/garment.asp

New York has the most lax laws of the three. Registration fees are $200 for manufacturers with a $150 annual renewal. The main purpose of New York's law is to regulate the factories and to ensure all factory workers are paid fair wages. The NY labor board hosts an online directory of registered factories. This might be a good place to start when searching for a factory in the state of New York.

Chapter 37
Product Safety Regulations

The latest law affecting you as a manufacturer has to do with product safety. It was passed in early 2008 and became effective on November 6, 2008. It is called the Consumer Products Safety Improvement Act (CPSIA). The law was passed to protect children against recent problems with children's products.

Unfortunately, the law was not clearly written and contains many calls for confusion. Revisions to this act are being made on a weekly basis, so by the time this book is in print, more information will be available. I recommend checking the Consumer Products Safety Commission (CPSC) website for more information.

The law targets manufacturers of products intended for use of children age 12 and under. This affects all children's' product and garment manufacturers based on lead and phthalate content; dyes, buttons, swarovski crystals, zippers and several other embellishments may contain trace levels of lead, so these levels must be tested for compliance.

Consumer Products Safety Improvement Act:
http://www.cpsc.gov/ about/cpsia/legislation. html#summaries

Consumer Products Safety Commission:
www.cpsc.gov

Notes:

RUNNING YOUR BUSINESS

Chapter 38
Employees and Contractors

Your business is up and running, demand for your product is up, and you discover that you can no longer do all the work yourself and you need help. Congratulations. Knowing you cannot do everything yourself and you need to hire help is the first key to success. So, when is the right time to hire employees and how do you do it? First let's see what kind of help you can get, and what you are responsible for with each.

- **Employees:** You must withhold federal, state and city (where applicable), social security and Medicare taxes, match social security, pay workers compensation insurance (where applicable), and pay unemployment taxes. You must do all this on a set schedule and comply with a number of state and federal employee regulations. You must issue a W-2 form annually.

- **Independent Contractors:** Independent contractors pay their own taxes. You hire them for a specific task and pay them an agreed to dollar amount, typically per hour. You

Employer's Tax Guide, IRS Publication 15:
http://www.irs.gov/pub/irs-pdf/p15.pdf

Notes:

report your payments to them on a Form 1099 (for payments over $600 a year).

Internal Revenue Service Business Guidelines:
irs.gov/businesses

Naturally, you must be asking, "Why would I want to hire an employee, with all the tax work involved?" The Internal Revenue Service has rules as to who can qualify as an independent contractor and who is an employee. By IRS definition:

Notes:

> "The general rule is that an individual is an **independent contractor** if (the person for whom the services are performed) has the right to control or direct only the result of the work, ***and not what will be done and how it will be done or method of accomplishing the result.***

> "People such as lawyers, contractors, subcontractors, public stenographers, and auctioneers who follow an independent trade, business, or profession in which they offer their services to the public, are **generally** not employees. However, whether such people are employees or independent contractors depends on the facts in each case."

As you can see, the criterion IRS uses is "Can you or can you not control the work of the person working for you." If the answer is yes, then the person is an employee, if no, you have an independent contractor. There are stiff penalties for treating employees as independent contractors, so be honest in your assessment.

In the fashion industry, you're more likely to deal with independent contractors rather than employees. A person you hire for his or her trade skill, such as a patternmaker, sample maker, or a web designer, is usually an independent contractor. Hiring an administrative assistant for day-to-day operations would be considered an employee.

If you are unable to figure out whether an individual falls into the employee or independent contractor category, the IRS has a helpful Form SS-8, "Determination of Worker Status for Purposes of Federal Employment Taxes and Income Tax Withholding." If you can to say the name of this form three times in a row without stumbling, give yourself a lollipop.

Form SS-8:
http://www.irs.gov/pub/
irs-pdf/fss8.pdf

Because independent contractors are self-employed and require little obligation on your part, their pay rates are much higher than employee wages. This is true for two reasons. 1. They must pay self-employment taxes. 2. They are saving you time and money, because you don't have to collect and report federal, social security and other taxes, or pay workers compensation and unemployment taxes as you would for employees.

Notes:

If an independent contractor you hire earns more than $600 from you, you are required to issue them a Form 1099 at the end of the year reporting the amount you paid them. The contractor will then pay taxes on that amount.

Let's say that after reading this, you conclude that you want complete control over how and where the work is performed and you decide to hire an employee. Here is a list of steps you need to take to ensure that you set this up properly.

• Have your employee fill out Form W-4 (Employee's Withholding Allowance Certificate), Form I-9 (Employment

Notes:

Eligibility Verification), and Form W-5 (Earned Income Credit Advanced Payment Certificate) if applicable. In some states, you must mail copies of these forms to your state government offices and in others, these forms stay in your possession. You use this information to properly withhold the necessary taxes.

- Register with your state's new hire reporting program within 20 days of hire or rehire. Check with your state on specific requirements.

- Sign up for Worker's Compensation Insurance

- Register to start paying Unemployment Insurance Tax (file with U.S. Department of Labor)

- Obtain disability insurance if required by your state

- Post workplace notices

- File IRS Form 941 to choose whether to report and pay the withholding monthly, quarterly or annually.

Unemployment
Insurance Tax:
http://workforcesecurity.
doleta.gov/unemploy/
uitaxtopic.asp

To find out more on your state's specific requirements for employers, check your secretary of state's website and search under small business. The IRS and the Department of Labor also have great resources and more forms than you could ever imagine existed.

Chapter 39
Budgeting Basics

Budgeting your finances may seem daunting, but taking the proper steps will help you see profits in your future. A few words of encouragement before we delve into the nitty-gritty of it. Look forward to your growth. If you plan out your finances and your time well, you should expect your business to grow exponentially by your second year. You are starting at a $0 profit, so growth must be grand.

In your first year of business, you will be busy creating your collections, building your marketing campaign, and learning from your mistakes. But your second year, your business should have grown considerably in assets, inventory, and status. This does not mean that you will be <u>in the black</u> in year two; you may not even see an actual profit until year three or even later. But if you invest your time well, follow the advice in this book, and don't lose sign of your vision, it will happen.

I cannot stress enough how important it is to keep to your budget. It's easy to rationalize spending just a little extra, but it can quickly become a habit. Set limits to your expenses. Simply put, a budget is planning on how to meet your expenses.

Notes:

_____

_____

_____

_____

_____

_____

In the Black:
making a profit. When revenue exceeds expenses

Notes:

Your first year of business will incur several expenses that will usually not re-occur on an annual basis, these are your start-up costs. In an on going basis, there are two major kinds of expenses, variable and fixed. Your variable cost is determined by what you actually produce. Your fixed costs are the costs you incur to run your business.

Fixed costs can be separated into two categories: direct and indirect. Direct fixed expenses include product development, photography and tradeshow expenses. Indirect fixed expenses are your monthly expenses, or overhead. In the following chapters, I elaborate on each of these costs.

Chapter 40
Start-up Costs

Let's get this party started right! In order to get started correctly, we need to determine what your start-up expenses will be. Your start-up costs are one-time expenses that happen in your first year of business. These can include setting up your business entity, legal fees, logo development and the list goes on.

I've outlined several expenses that may apply to your business, but don't limit yourself to this list. You will need to create a detailed list of start-up expenses for your business planning.

- **Business Entity –** Set up your business entity legally.

- **Branding and Logo Development –** If you plan to hire a professional to get your company image set up, include that in your start-up costs.

- **Garment Registration –** Register with your state's labor board, if applicable.

- **Equipment –** This includes equipment that you will need to purchase to operate your business successfully: sewing machines, computers, printers, phones and fax. This does

Notes:

Notes:

not include items you already own, although you should also create an inventory list of equipment and tools you plan to contribute to your business.

- **Licenses and Permits –** This includes the cost to register your business, get your resale number and any other permits you need.

- **Legal Fees** – Budget for a legal business setup if you plan on operating as an entity other than a sole proprietorship. If you are seeking a trademark or patent, an intellectual property law professional may be necessary. These fees will vary vastly based on what you are looking for.

- **Technology –** Consider purchasing bookkeeping software, graphic software as well as any other software needed to properly run your business.

- **Website** – A nicely designed website can range anywhere from $500 to $5,000, depending of your requirements.

Start Up Cost

	Cost
Business Entity	
Branding & Logo	
Garment Registration	
Equipment	
Licenses & Permits	
Legal Fees	
Technology	
Website	
Total Start-Up Cost	$

Inventory of Contributed Assets

Inventory Item	Price
Total Inventory Investment	$

Chapter 41
Variable Costs

After determining your start up costs, the next stage in developing your budget is to calculate the basis of your variable costs. Your variable costs are your costs of production. To determine this you first need to determine your cost of goods. In the fashion industry, this process is generally described as costing.

Cost of Goods

To figure out the actual cost of your garment in terms of materials, you will need to know the cost of fabric per yard and how many yards it takes to make your product, your patternmaker should be able to help you in determining the exact amount.

You also need to know what it will cost to have the garments cut and sewn. For your first production run, you should shop around for the manufacturer who is right for your product. Some contractors will have large minimums (for example, 1000 pieces) and some may have smaller requirements (as few as 25). Get sewing quotes for both.

If you are going to start with a small production run, you may also want to find out how much it would cost to hire an

Notes:

Notes:

independent seamstress. Remember, every case scenario and its cost must be considered! This last quote could be important if you get a large enough order that you can't handle personally, but small enough that a contactor won't touch it.

Use the higher quotes when figuring your costs, and price your garments accordingly. As a design company, it is always easier to lower your prices once you establish yourself, but harder to raise them and still keep your clientele. Start high and go down. This can really save you in the end. Unexpected expenses and emergencies always pop up at the most inopportune moments and its better to have some financial leeway to meet them.

Other than your cost of fabric and sewing, there are a few other expenses you need to take into account when costing your garments. These can include your sewn-in label, cutting costs, dying costs and your notions, such as zippers, elastic, and buttons. Your sewing quotes should include the attachment of these items, although certain exceptions may apply when attaching grommets, eyelets and buttonholes, so get those quotes as well.

Hot Tip!

Woven labels are more costly and many people cut them out. Printed labels are softer, are less likely to be cut out, but may not look as professional. Choose the label that is the most appropriate for your line.

Production Cost

Calculating your budget for production is directly linked to the amount of sales you expect. If you expect to sell 100 units wholesale to a retailer, then you will have to produce 100 units, right? Almost. You should figure that up to 5% of the pieces produced may be flawed and unsellable. Add that percentage to the numbers you produce.

If you plan on selling directly to the consumer through fairs or a website, you will need to produce enough inventory to handle orders and direct sales. One more thing to consider, if your product is a best seller, will you have inventory available for re-orders? Let's lump these two scenarios together and estimate that you wish to produce an additional 10% of inventory.

Now for our first production calculation. Let's calculate production costs for one garment of your collection. You will need to create separate production cost sheets for each garment you are producing – a sample is included at the end of the chapter.

Let's assume you are going to produce 100 pieces of one garment to fill orders that were placed, an additional 5% for damaged, plus another 10% for direct sales through your website.

100 pieces x 5% = 5 (Damaged allowance)
100 pieces x 10% = 10 (Allowance for direct sales and reorders)

Your production quantity is 115 pieces. In your cost sheet, fill out the costs for this garment (fabric, trims, sewing, and cutting) and multiply by your quantity (115). This is your production cost for this garment.

Notes:

This is an example of a cost sheet similar to one I use in my business. You will need to fill one out for each item you design and develop. Please note that your cost sheet should be customized to accommodate your own business needs.

Cost Sheet

Style # _____   **Style Name:** _____   **Season:** _____

TECHNICAL FLAT

Fabric	Cost Per Yard	Yardage	Total Cost
Self			
Contrast			
Lining			
Interfacing			

Notions	Cost Per Piece	Quantity Used	Total Cost
Zipper			
Buttons			
Hook & Eye			
Label			
		Materials Cost	
		Sewing Cost	
		Cutting Cost	
		Dying Cost	
		Total Cost	

To properly cost out your production, you will need to fill out one garment production cost worksheet for each design you are producing. In the lower form, compile all your garment worksheets to receive an accurate assessment for your total production costs.

Garment Production Cost Worksheet

Style #: ....

Style Name: ....

Season: ....

Number of items ordered	
__% Allowance for damaged goods	
__%Allowance for direct sales	
Total items to be produced	

Production Cost

Cost of Goods per Piece	
Total quantity produced	X
Total Production Cost	

Collection Production Cost Worksheet

Season: ....

	Production Cost
Style #	
Style #	
Style #	
Style #	
Style #	
Total Production Cost	$

Chapter 42
Direct Fixed Costs

At first glance, you may think that items such as development and photography are variable costs. In actuality, these items are examples of fixed costs directly related to each collection you produce. Direct fixed costs are linked to your production cycles. Depending on the number of collections you produce, these costs will vary from year to year. Let's break everything down to create a per collection budget.

Development Cost

The most complex direct fixed cost is your development cost. Your initial collection will be the most expensive to develop. You will be creating your <u>blocks</u> and hashing out your fit issues with your patternmaker. With your second, third, and fourth collections you should see a reduction in these costs. You shouldn't have to redevelop your blocks unless you had major issues in your first collection.

Designers often re-release the same silhouette in more than one collection but offer that design in a different fabric or color. In this case, you won't need to recalculate costs for the pattern work and development of the sample, just the sample itself.

Notes:

Blocks: *basic pattern for each size and type of garment. You will generally create a basic skirt, bodice, torso, sleeve and pant pattern to be used in drafting each pattern in your collection.*

Notes:

Below is a general breakdown of costs for the development of each piece.

- **Fabric cost** for creating all samples of that garment. Calculate for the number of samples you expect to generate, including working samples and production samples.
- **Trim cost** for samples. Calculate this in the same manner as your fabric costs.
- **Sample sewing**—Decide how much you plan to spend on each sample and the number of samples. Consider, if you do not get a good working sample after you've reached your budget, to either drop the design or get a new sample/pattern maker.
- **Pattern**—You may want to combine the sample sewing with your pattern work in your development cost if you have one contractor do both of them.
- **Grading services** - Include costs for digitizing, grading, and marking services.

Development Cost

Style #: _____

Style Name: _____

	Cost
Fabric	
Trim	
Pattern Development	
Sample Sewing	
Grading	
Fittings	
Total Development Cost	

Photography Cost

You may need to photograph your collection before you start to sell it. These photos can be used to produce a look book, enhance your website or advertise your business. This needs to be budgeted for every collection you create.

The most obvious expense in photography is hiring a photographer and a model. As an independent designer, we need to be resourceful and use the services available to us. One way to acquire professional photos is to enter into a TFP (Time for Prints) or TFCD (Time for CDs) arrangement. Many models and photographers are eager to build their portfolios and jump at the opportunity to photograph unique clothing. This arrangement gives everyone in the agreement rights to use the photos with limited expenses. You get your model shots, and everyone gets images for their own use.

To legally use these photos in print or online, you need to have everyone involved sign releases to use the photos. Some releases require all parties' names to be disclosed with the photos. It is to your benefit that you require your company name linked with all photos of your designs.

You may not always receive images that work for you from a TFP/TFCD photo shoot, so it may be worth an investment to hire a photographer or a model for the shoot. Sometimes you may require a makeup artist or hairstylist to achieve a specific look. Other expenses that may occur as a photography expense are any Photoshop work done by the photographer.

Notes:

TFP/TFCD resource: modelmayhem.com, craigslist.org

Notes:

Other Collection Costs

Many other costs may occur in conjunction with releasing a collection. Here are a few examples of other direct fixed costs.

- **Printing, Design and Layout –** Look book and line sheets should look professional. Consider hiring a professional to design the layout for each of these.

- **Tradeshows** – Tradeshows contain many expenses besides the space fees. Load in and load out expenses, hotel, food and transportation all need to be factored in. Don't forget your display expenses.

- **Website** – Your website should be updated with each collection.

Direct Fixed Cost Per Collection

Season:_____

Development Cost for Entire Collection

Style #	
Style #	
Style #	
Style #	
Style #	
Total Development Cost	$

Photography Cost

Photographer	
Model	
Makeup Artist	
Hair Stylist	
Photoshop	
Prints	
Total Photography Cost	$

Tradeshow Cost

Show Fee	
Load in/load out	
Display	
Hotel	
Food	
Airfare	
Car Rental	
Total Tradeshow Cost	$

Other Collection Costs

Printing	
Print Design & Layout	
Website	
Total Other Collection Costs	$

Total Direct Fixed Cost	$

Chapter 43
Indirect Fixed Expenses

Indirect fixed expenses are everything that it takes to keep your business open each month: rent, website hosting fees, salaries, and the like. These expenses can also be referred to as overhead. These are indirect fixed expenses because they do not directly relate to number of collection you produce or the revenue you receive.

Below are several indirect fixed expenses typical for a fashion business. These may not exactly match your expenses, but they will help you in determining your own fixed costs. I have broken down the fixed expenses into administrative, marketing & sales, rent and labor.

Administrative

- **Accounting** – The price of accounting services can vary vastly depending on where you live. In larger metropolitan areas, a good accountant can charge about $600 for an annual tax filing. Ask for referrals from friends and colleagues to find a good one. There are accountants who

Notes:

Notes:

specialize in the apparel business, but any good accountant can do the job. Don't skimp on an accounting service. If you've ever done your own taxes, you know how long it can take. Now that you have your own business, your time is valuable and spending those few extra dollars to get your taxes filed properly will free you up from this tedious task and let you focus on other work.

- **Bookkeeping** – The price of a bookkeeper can vary, but a good one will update your books on a monthly basis. You may want to consider hiring your bookkeeper to show you how to do your books yourself. You can invest in a program like QuickBooks if you want to do your bookkeeping yourself, but make sure you have time to learn. If you do your own books you will be able to run reports at any time to track your business progress. And let's be honest; it's sometimes hard to trust someone else with your personal and professional finances, especially if you're a small business.

- **Business License & Renewals** – Registration and license renewals are usually fixed costs you must include in your annual budget. Although these may not occur monthly, they are annual recurring expenses that do not vary depending on your revenue.

- **Credit Card/Bank Charges** – If you will be processing credit cards, which is likely, there are monthly fees linked to these. This is usually a flat monthly rate, plus a percentage of the processed amount. The bank where you opened your checking account most likely has merchant services, so check with them first. Questions to ask yourself when considering credit card services are: 1.Will you be processing orders online? 2. Does your internet service offer online processing?

3. Can you use a <u>virtual terminal</u>, or do you need an actual one? If you will only be taking wholesale orders and selling online, you do not need a terminal.

If you need to process orders at events, street fairs or trunk shows, a virtual terminal will do just fine. You'll record the customers' information manually and run the cards later. This does not guarantee that every sale will go through, due to maxed out cards or incorrectly recorded information.

Hot Tip!

To help guarantee that all your sales will go through, you should take phone numbers and run the sales immediately after you get home. Shoppers sometimes overspend and max out cards at shopping events. Nine times out of ten, if a card doesn't go through and you call, the customer will get back to you.

- **Equipment Rental** – Include equipment rental fees in your budget if you are leasing or paying in installments. This may include a credit card terminal, a copy machine or postage meter.

- **Office Supplies** – For me, $100 monthly usually covers my office supplies, including the short-lived ink cartridges that my printer sucks up. You know your own spending, so budget accordingly.

- **Postage & Shipping** – Account for shipping your products, as well as any office mailings. If you are selling online, you might

Virtual terminal: a credit card processing service that does not require a physical terminal, but an internet connection

Notes:

Notes:

want to charge the customer a small handling fee to cover your shipping cost and the various related service charges. When shipping merchandise to retailers, it is common practice to charge them for it.

- **Telephone** – Budget for any designated phone or fax lines for your business, and your cell phone. You can save here by setting up a fax number through a fax-to-email service.

- **Utilities** – Figure these for any rented space, as well as your home office if you have one. You will figure the percentage your office takes up in your home and calculate your costs based on it. You can cut costs here by working in the dark (just kidding).

Marketing & Sales

- **Advertising** – You will want to try different advertising approaches. See what brings you the largest response. Large advertising campaigns can be costly, so carry over to the next month any amount budgeted each month that you don't use.

- **Event Fees** – Do you plan on participating in street fairs or sample sales? Include all events you plan on selling at.

- **Printed Materials** – Business cards you usually need to order once or twice a year. Other printed materials include postcards, line sheets and look books.

Car Share Programs:
citycarshare.org,
zipcar.com

- **Travel** – Keep track of your business mileage and gas usage and use it to make projections to use for next month or next year. Don't forget your auto insurance. If you really want to cut car costs, and you live in a large metropolitan area, you may be able to use a car share program. You pay a flat hourly fee for the car and your gas and insurance is included. To budget, you will need to know the fee and the number of hours you use your car for business. Check out CityCar Share and Zip Car.

Hot Tip!

Carpool on fabric buying trips if you can. It's cheaper and more fun. If renting instead of using your own car, waive the insurance. What most credit card companies don't tell you is that they insure the car you rent so you don't need to buy any extra insurance. Make sure your credit card company offers this before renting a car.

- **Website** – You need to include in your budget your hosting service monthly fee, annual domain name renewals, and any other charges associated with maintaining your website.

Rent

- **Rent** – If you are renting a studio, this would be your main budget item. In some areas, it may only cost you a few hundred dollars for a decent studio space. Don't go for more than what you really need. Because you're not running a store, location isn't as important, so don't overpay for a fabulous location. Try to avoid signing any long term leases, you don't know where your business will go.

- **Insurance** – Call the company that insures your home or car and ask if they will cover your business. If not, they may be able to refer you to someone. Budget about $100-$150 a month until you get your actual quote.

Notes:

Notes:

Now that you have a general idea of what some of your fixed expenses could be, you can start to build your budget for your first year. (Don't forget to multiply monthly costs by 12 for your total annual budget.) In the second and third year, most amounts will increase. On average, with inflation, you can guess that your expenses will grow up to 10% annually.

Labor

Labor expenses are the most important kind of expenses, but are frequently overlooked. As a small business owner, a common misconception is that our salary is our business profits. It sounds realistic enough, but what if we don't see a profit until our third year? How do you plan on supporting yourself? If you are approaching this business as a part-time gig or as a hobby, this may make sense. But for the rest of us, we would like to receive payment for our efforts. Build a salary for yourself into your indirect fixed costs.

- **Principal Salary** – Would you work 80 hours a week for a mere $25,000 a year? I doubt it. Give yourself a salary that reflects the work you do. If you are working on your business 10 hours a week, maybe a $25,000 salary makes sense, but if you are serious about making your business a success, factor in a salary of $40,000 to $50,000 annually.

- **Assistants** – Follow the guidelines we discussed in Chapter 38: Employees and Contractors.

Indirect Fixed Costs

	Monthly Estimate
Administrative	
Accounting	
Bookkeeping	
Business License Renewals	
Credit Card & Bank Charges	
Equipment Rental	
Office Supplies	
Postage & Shipping	
Telephone	
Utilities	
Total Administrative Costs	$
Marketing & Sales	
Advertising	
Event Fees	
Printed Material	
Travel	
Vehicle Expenses	
Website	
Total Marketing & Sales Costs	$
Rent	
Rent	
Insurance	
Total Rental Costs	$
Labor	
Principal	
Assistant	
Total Labor Costs	$
Total Indirect Fixed Costs	$

Chapter 44
Pricing

We are at the point where we need to determine our <u>wholesale price</u> in order to make our profit happen. In old school days, keystone pricing was the most common method used in determining a wholesale price. Keystoning is doubling the cost of goods. I strongly disagree with following this practice for many reasons. As an independent designer we do not produce the quantities to ever create a profit using this method.

Determining your wholesale prices shouldn't be as simple as just doubling your cost. Let me explain why. Have you thought about where the money is coming from to cover your overhead, salary and those direct fixed costs? Yes, I said salary. You must not forget your number one reason for going into business for yourself—to make a living from it.

If you've started adding up the numbers yet, you may start to realize you may need to sell well over 5,000 items just to recoup your costs, but let's not get ahead of ourselves.

Wholesale Price:
The price offered to retailers. This price is not available to consumers

Notes:

Notes:

Wholesale Pricing

Let's start out basic and work out the complicated stuff in a minute. We need to use the information we compiled in the previous four chapters:

Chapter 40: Start-Up Costs & Current Assets
Why might you calculate this into your wholesale price? **All** expenses need to be considered in determining your pricing. This will ensure that your profits won't be eaten for dinner. A better question to ask is, "How is this calculated?" This bit is a little complicated, but you can take the resulted numbers and plug them directly into your 5-year projections.

In the finance world, start-up costs are also referred to as a "Goodwill Investment." Even though these expenses occur in the start of your business, the actual expense is usually amortized over 30 years, meaning the expense is spread out equally over 30 years. A similar process occurs with your contributed assets. Your assets are depreciated over 10 to 15 years. This also means you can't claim it on your taxes in one lump sum. You will need to check with your accountant to determine these specific items. For calculation purposes only, we will use 15 years for depreciation and 30 years for start-up costs. These expenses become part of your indirect fixed expenses.

____ (Start-up Costs)/30 years/12 months = ____ Monthly
____ (Inventory Assets)/15 years/12 months = ____ Monthly

Chapter 41: Variable Costs
You will need your cost of goods calculated for each item in your collection as well as your production estimates. This

quantity of production will be used in the next steps.

Chapter 42: Direct Fixed Cost
You need the total direct fixed costs calculated. Make estimations from your research to fill this section out fully. To determine the amount you need to factor into your wholesale price, divide your total direct fixed cost by the quantity planned for production.

___ Direct Costs/___ Quantity

Chapter 43: Indirect Fixed Cost
You will need to make good faith estimates for these expenses as well. Don't forget your salary (I can't stress this enough). Take your total annual indirect fixed expenses and divide them by the quantity you plan to produce.

(___ Indirect Monthly Cost x 12 Months)/___ Quantity

If you plan to produce more than one collection per year, you can alter this amount to reflect a production cycle, but remember that your first year will be your most expensive, so defaulting to a year as opposed to a production cycle may ensure a little wiggle room for future pricing. It is easy to lower prices after establishing your business, but difficult to raise them. Raising prices can result in lost customers and retailers.

You have now acquired all the information needed to calculate your wholesale price minus one important factor, profit. Add your cost of goods to your per piece direct and indirect expenses. Get your total then add your desired profit. A reasonable profit for this industry is 35%, but play around

Notes:

Notes:

with the percentages to see what profits you can yield. Your final step is to add up each of these totals, resulting in your wholesale price.

(__ Cost of Goods + __ Direct Cost + __ Indirect Cost) x __% = Profit

__ Profit + __ Cost of Goods + __ Direct Cost + __ Indirect Cost = Wholesale

Is it safe to say that my dislike for keystoning is valid? Prove me wrong, take your cost of goods and double it. Does that total come close to covering all your expenses? Taking this approach will ensure you make a profit, take a salary and cover all your expenses.

To accurately calculate these formulas, I recommend developing an Excel spreadsheet that will update your amounts automatically.

Retail Pricing

Here's your next wake up call. The retail markup is going to be anywhere from two to three times of what the retailer paid for your product wholesale. The retailer needs to ensure they cover all their operating expenses in their markup, as you did your own.

I offer a recommended retail price to my stores at 2.5 times my wholesale price. You can use this amount as a base if you plan on selling your collection directly to the public. It is important to accurately assume a reasonable markup. Your biggest downfall can happen if you undercut your retailers and sell your merchandise at a lower price. This will discourage stores from re-ordering or purchasing future collections.

Looking back to your original goals when you began reading this book, does your product still fit the price point and customer you defined? If your answer is no, you have some serious re-evaluating to do. Where can you cut your costs? That answer is usually in the fabric and your pattern. If your product has 10 pattern pieces and you could change it to seven pattern pieces without compromising your vision; your sewing and cutting cost will both be lowered. Hoping you have a great relationship with your pattern maker, ask her for advice on how to cut the costs for production. A good patternmaker will usually have ideas for pattern changes.

If you have re-evaluated your costs, made your changes across the board, and the retail price is still too high for your market or customer, maybe its time to re-evaluate who your customer is. Is it possible that the customer you had planned to target is not the customer you are reaching?

Flexibility in changing your customer is a must, especially if you are not willing to budge on your design. At this point you will need to go back to the beginning, review your target customer and market, and make adjustments. If you do not do this now, you will end up paying severely in time and money in the long run. It could affect the tradeshow you plan on attending, the stores you plan on selling to, and your entire marketing campaign.

Notes:

Pricing

Style #	Quantity to be Produced	Cost of Goods	Direct Fixed Cost	Indirect Fixed Cost	Total Cost	Profit	Wholesale Price
Total Quantity							

Direct Fixed Cost

Total Direct Fixed Cost	
Divided by Total Quantity	/
Total Direct Cost Per Garment	

Indirect Fixed Cost (Annual – multiply monthly by 12)

Indirect Fixed Cost	
Amortized Startup Cost	
Depreciated Assets	
Total Fixed Costs	
Divided by Total Quantity	/
Total Indirect Fixed Cost	

Chapter 45
Financial Projections

Overwhelmed yet?

Projecting the financial future of your business is a good faith estimate and you need to be realistic. You will need to project your financials for not only your business plan, but for your own business goals. If you are too modest in your projections, no financier will look at you. The same is true if your estimate is unrealistically high. Every dollar amount in your projections needs to be backed up by your plans for the future. If you do not plan any advertising, trade shows, or marketing, and you calculate that you will be doing one million dollars in sales by the third year, you need to wake up.

To do a financial projection, you need to make reasonable assumptions on how many sales you will have, how many stores will carry your merchandise, and how you plan on reaching these goals. Create a timeline of your goals to make them realistic and within reach. Set marketing, advertising and tradeshow goals. This will help you achieve a visual picture of where your revenue is coming from.

One way to determine your projected sales for each year is by planning the expectations of your first collection. Calculate

Notes:

Notes:

in a percentage of growth for sequential years and relate this directly to your first collection and production costs. This part can get pretty complicated, pretty fast. If you are pretty handy using Excel and math, you shouldn't have a problem figuring this out. But if you are staring blankly at this book right now, I might have a handy tool for you to use.

In a previous career, I worked in computer programming and document automation. I brought these problem solving, analytical, and mathematical skills into creating my own financial projection worksheet in Excel. I link everything of discussion in this section into a handy "plug and play" worksheet. If you are interested in acquiring a copy for yourself, see our website EastBayFashionResource.com for more details.

Included here are blank financial projection worksheets for one year and for 5 years. Plan on explaining why and how you came to these dollar amounts in your business plan.

One Year Financial Projections

	January	February	March	April	May	June	July	August	September	October	November	December
Revenues												
Wholesale												
Retail												
Total Revenue												
Direct Fixed Expenses												
Development												
Photography												
Printing, Design & Layout												
Tradeshow												
Website												
Indirect Fixed Expenses												
Administrative												
Marketing & Sales												
Rent												
Labor												
Principal Salary												
Assistant												
Total Expenses												
Net Income												

Five Year Financial Projections

	Year 1	Year 2	Year 3	Year 4	Year 5
Revenues					
Wholesale					
Retail					
Total Revenue					
Direct Fixed Expenses					
Development					
Photography					
Printing, Design & Layout					
Tradeshow					
Website					
Indirect Fixed Expenses					
Administrative					
Marketing & Sales					
Rent					
Labor					
Principal Salary					
Assistant					
Total Expenses					
	-	-	-	-	-
Net Income					

Chapter 46
Break Even Point

What is the break even point? It is the point where your sales match your expenses. "Breaking even" does not mean you are making a profit, only that you're not losing any money.

To figure your break even point, calculate how much it costs for you to be in business each month (your direct and indirect fixed costs). Let's just say that amount is $2000. You may think that you need to sell $2000 in merchandise to break even. Wrong.

If you think this way, you will go broke faster than a shop-aholic with *The Home Shopping Network*. You forgot to include your cost of goods (COG) for the merchandise that you sold. To make our lives easy, let's just say your COG for that $2000 of merchandise is $1000. So then, does it make sense to say that it takes $3000 in sales to break even each month? No.

Calculating your Break Even Point

Instead of spending hours going back and forth with how much you need to sell in order to break even, let's create a mathematical formula to figure it out for us. We need to first calculate our Gross Profit Margin (GPM).

Notes:

Notes:

Your GPM is the percentage of markup from the Cost of Goods to wholesale. You can only calculate this once you cost your garment and figure out your wholesale pricing. Based on my pricing method, this will vary for each item. To be precise, you can calculate the average of the projected quantities, but that becomes very complicated. I would recommend determining your GPM for each product and use the lowest percentage of the batch to calculate your Break Even Point. This will yield the most conservative numbers.

Divide your Cost of Goods (COG) by your Wholesale Price. Then subtract that percentage from 100% and that number is your Gross Profit Margin.

Example: The COG for a skirt is $6.50 and was marked up to $25 for wholesale.

$6.50 cost of goods/$25 wholesale price = .26 or 26%

100% – 26% = **74% Gross Profit Margin**

Let us now calculate the Break Even Point. Take your average direct and indirect fixed cost for one month (which we will say is $5000) and divide it by the GPM (turn the percentage into a decimal point).

Example: $5000 Fixed Cost / .74 Gross Profit Margin (in decimal form) = **$6,756.76 Break Even Point**

Back to a question from earlier. When do you make a profit? When you exceed your Break Even Point. To determine when your business breaks even, add your accumulated losses from each month and offset them from your revenues, when you hit zero, your business has broken even. Your actual break even point may not occur until your second year of business or later.

Break Even Point

Style #: ....

Cost of Goods	
Wholesale Price	/
Total Cost of Goods Percentage	

	100%
Cost of Goods Percentage	-
Total Gross Profit Margin	

Style #: ....

Cost of Goods	
Wholesale Price	/
Total Cost of Goods Percentage	

	100%
Cost of Goods Percentage	-
Total Gross Profit Margin	

Style #: ....

Cost of Goods	
Wholesale Price	/
Total Cost of Goods Percentage	

	100%
Cost of Goods Percentage	-
Total Gross Profit Margin	

Of the above Gross Profit Margins calculated, use your smallest percentage in the following calculation.

Fixed Monthly Cost	
Gross Profit Margin (decimal form)	/
Total Break Even Point	

Chapter 47
Exit Strategy

Exit strategies are not there to discourage you, but to help you plan on what you want to do 2, 5, 10 or 20 years down the road. An exit strategy needs to be in your business plan to show a lender what you plan on doing in the future.

Planning your exit strategy when you are planning your launch might seem a little crazy, but you should really consider who will take over your business when it comes time for you to retire. Do you have plans to build up your business in 3 years then to sell it off? Do you want to sell when you reach a certain sales revenue? Do you want your children to continue a tradition you've build? Investors, partners and financiers are all interested in your plans.

Here are some ways to exit a business endeavor:
• Sell your business
• Pass it on to family
• Take your business public and sell shares
• Dissolve your business.

Unfortunately, most design businesses exit via the last option, but I have faith in you that you will follow the lead and choose the first option and sell your business.

Notes:

BUILDING A BUSINESS PLAN

Chapter 48
Introduction to Your Business Plan

So what can you do with all the information you've read up to this point? Organize it into your very own business plan. I've provided a general outline for a business plan, as well as a top secret business plan for your reference. Use them and everything else you've learned from this book to write your own business plan.

Your business plan is not only your map for the future, but your tool for raising capital as well. Even if you do not plan to use a business plan to seek funding, you should make one for yourself. It can be a very useful tool for helping you stick to your goals and your budget. Update it often and include figures as years pass to track your growth.

The plan featured here is my own business plan recently revised for the current year in operation. I have removed some personal information, some financials, but other than that, this is the plan I operate my business by, and you can use it as a reference. Use your own language to write your own business plan. Everything will vary for your own business, so be specific in your descriptions and tailor it to your own line.

Notes:

Chapter 49
Cover Page

Use a clear format and be straight to the point. Include your company name, logo, address, web address, email, phone number, and the names of all of the owners.

Porcelynne Lingerie

Business Plan

Jennifer Lynne Matthews
261 10th Street #302
Oakland, CA 94607
510-834-8443

www.porcelynne.com
jennifer@porcelynne.com

Chapter 50
Executive Summary

The executive summary is a general summary of everything that is discussed in the remainder of the business plan and is generally written last. This is also the area where you should state the amount of funding you're requesting.

Executive Summary

Porcelynne Lingerie, a manufacturer of intimate apparel is strategically situated to expand its internet and boutique distribution to nationwide. The firm's reputation for developing stylish, comfortable and environmentally friendly undergarments account for its part and future growth.

Porcelynne Lingerie's business plan provides details as to its product development, manufacturing and wholesale/retail distribution efforts. The unique mixture of product materials and manufacturing supports a break even point after year one and a recovery of all production costs by the end of year two. Profit projections in year three are shown at 20% assumption anticipated growth in production and sales.

These projections demonstrate an ability to repay a business loan of $100,000 over three years.

Chapter 51
Objectives

This section of the plan describes the objectives of your business. Here, you will evaluate what is already out in the market you want to target and where your product will fit in it. You will offer your own research, the current size and future direction of the market and your business.

Objectives

Mission Statement

Porcelynne Lingerie develops and manufactures comfortable, quality and environmentally friendly intimate apparel. Our fit is unique and has been developed over the course of many years in researching women needs for the undergarment. Our specially chosen bamboo fabrics are not only the softest fabrics in today's market, but they also hold special antibacterial properties conducive to intimate apparel.

Target Market

Our moderate price point targets our market to be that of independent designer boutiques, salons and spas. Retail prices range from $45 to $75. Most pieces in our collection are sold as a set, averaging a purchase at $120. Studies show that in our target audience, women tend to purchase 8 to 10 pieces of lingerie each year. They retain use for approximately 3 years and generally have a couple dozen pieces in their dressers.

Market Growth

According to "The USA Intimate Apparel Market Research Report" published in January 2008 by Infomat, Inc., "Intimate apparel is now a $9.6 billion dollar industry, up nearly 4% from previous years. Total apparel sales have reached up to $181 billion with intimates and sleepwear helping to fuel growth." As stated in this report, this growth is expected to continue and increase up to 10% by 2010. Sales numbers are not specified to one particular market and cover all areas from budget to designer.

Company History

Porcelynne Lingerie began its business in 2002. In 2005, their "brick & mortar" boutique location opened in San Francisco. Two years later we began the process to re-focus our direction on expanding our clothing line and closed operations on the retail store location. The past six years gave us insight as to properly targeting our customer and market, as well as handling the demands of our public and building relationships with manufacturing facilities. During the past six years, we have received numbers of accolades in the form of press coverage and awards in the fashion industry. In 2005, we received the Best of San Francisco Mastermind award (SF Weekly) and in 2008, we received the Best of the East Bay (East Bay Express), to name a few.

Company Future

The five year focus for Porcelynne Lingerie plans to grow out of our small designer community and into the mass market and maintain our small designer appeal. We plan on using our historic success and press support as our major selling points to new retailers outside, enforcing our brand. Our first move to large scale is scheduled for 2009. We will be exhibiting at the Curve Tradeshow held in Las Vegas in February 2009 and August 2009. We are also launching a unique lace underwear design developed by a local artist and illustrator. In 2010, we plan on exhibiting in the Curve Tradeshows in both New York and Las Vegas.

It is through tradeshows like this and aggressive marketing and public relations strategies we will grow significantly in the next five years. Our expected growth may lead to the sale of Porcelynne Lingerie.

Chapter 52
Product

You will provide a detailed description of your products, fabrics and material used in production. This section lays out your development costs, product costs and your pricing.

Products

Porcelynne Lingerie produces intimate apparel, described as sports bras, tanks, tees, panties (briefs, boyshorts and thongs)

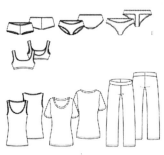

Materials

The majority of the designs in our collections are created out of a 95% Bamboo/5% Spandex blend. The collection is produced in a "prepared for dying" (PFD) state in manufacturing. Every piece is sewn first than is dyed according to the colors of the season. The process involves sending pre-made garments to a dye house for each color that was ordered.

Each season we will add new pieces to our collection. We are introducing a new piece for our collection for Fall 2009 release in a lace design. Working with artist and illustrator Ursula Young, we have developing an exclusive lace design for our most popular underwear design. By adding new pieces, we energize our sales and spread the cost of development over the year.

Development Cost

Our original development costs for our patterns and samples have been calculated based upon the previous collections and are no longer a current cost in our production. We start the 2009 year off with no additional cost of development for all current designs.

All future pattern development and samples will be conducted by our principal patternmaker, Jennifer Lynne. These costs for that service will be allocated over two collections, as most designs are reproduced from season to season in different fabrications. Development costs are broken down per piece by the quantity in production that is expected.

For example, if my development cost is $1,000 and I expect to produce 5,000 items for two separate collections, my development cost is broken down by 10,000 for a cost of 10 cents a piece.

Product Cost

The product cost consists of all materials, cutting, sewing and garment dying.

Cost of Goods

Style Name or Style Number	Total Cost of Goods	Cutting Cost	Sewing Cost	Garment Dying	Material Costs
Tank Top	$ 7.54	$ 0.75	$ 2.75	$ 0.75	$ 3.29
Tee Shirt	$ 9.61	$ 1.25	$ 3.25	$ 1.00	$ 4.11
Yoga Pants	$ 12.02	$ 1.25	$ 3.50	$ 1.00	$ 6.27
Sportsbra	$ 7.23	$ 1.00	$ 2.75	$ 0.75	$ 2.73
Boyshorts	$ 5.71	$ 0.50	$ 2.00	$ 0.50	$ 2.71
Brief	$ 5.96	$ 0.75	$ 2.00	$ 0.50	$ 2.71

See Appendix A for Breakdown of Materials Cost.

Wholesale Pricing

The wholesale price in the model consists of 4 costs: product cost, indirect fixed costs (an allocation of overhead), direct fixed costs (development, tradeshows and photography which occur for each collection) and a profit of 35%.

The model shows that a wholesale price of $22.00 yields a profit of $8.01.

Retail Pricing

Our suggested retail pricing is set at 2.5 times the wholesale price. Any merchandise we sell online or direct to consumer will be sold at our suggested retail price.

Style Name or Style Number	Suggested Retail Price	Wholesale	Profit	Indirect Fixed Cost	Direct Fixed Cost	Total Cost
Tank Top	$ 55.00	$ 22.00	$ 8.01	$ 6.01	$ 0.43	$ 7.54
Tee Shirt	$ 63.00	$ 25.00	$ 8.94	$ 6.01	$ 0.43	$ 9.61
Yoga Pants	$ 70.00	$ 28.00	$ 9.53	$ 6.01	$ 0.43	$ 12.02
Sportsbra	$ 53.00	$ 21.00	$ 7.33	$ 6.01	$ 0.43	$ 7.23
Boyshorts	$ 48.00	$ 19.00	$ 6.85	$ 6.01	$ 0.43	$ 5.71
Brief	$ 48.00	$ 19.00	$ 6.60	$ 6.01	$ 0.43	$ 5.96

Chapter 53
Marketing

This area of the plan you will describe where you see your target market geographically and what stores you see your products selling in.

Marketing

Customer and Market

Our target market reaches middle class women across America. According to buying reports posted in Women's Wear Daily, they spend approximately $5,000 annually on clothing. The share they spend on intimate apparel and active wear averages 10% of their clothing budget. Buying trends show her age ranges from 25 to 40 years old.

Our customer chooses comfort and fit over luxury name brands and is loyal with purchasing from independent designer boutiques. Our merchandise can be located in small shopping districts in suburban neighborhoods, spas and salons.

Distribution Channels

Direct Sales & Retail
Porcelynne Lingerie offers merchandise for retail sales directly to consumers through Porcelynne.com, through Etsy.com and Shopflick.com. They also offer retail shopping directly out of their showroom by appointment and at designated shopping events.

Wholesale
Our main wholesale channels are obtained at tradeshows. Direct mail marketing to retailers and press coverage secure additional accounts. When annual sales reach $300,000, we will seek sales representation of outside showrooms. This is estimated for our Fall 2010 collection. These sales reps will receive 15% commission for obtaining new accounts.

This is where you list your competition, your niche market and your sales strategy. How will word of your product get out? Who will be selling it? Sales Rep? In-house Rep? You? Trade Shows?

Competition

Three national competitors to Porcelynne Lingerie are Victoria's Secret, Hanky Panky and She&Me Intimates. The following chart details each company and whether Porcelynne shows strength or weakness for each factor.

Factor	Porcelynne	Strength	Weakness	Competitors		
				Victoria's Secret	Hanky Panky	She&Me Intimates
Products	Boyshort specialty, tanks, briefs, yoga pants, tees, sportsbras, thongs	Yes		Boyshorts, briefs, thongs, bras, sleepwear, outerwear	Thong and boyshorts	Boyshorts, briefs, sleep pants, tees, outerwear
Fabrics	High quality bamboo, moderate quality unique lace designs	Yes		Moderate quality – varies on style	Moderate quality lace	High quality modal and cottons
Price	Moderate		Yes	Moderate to Low	Moderate	Moderate to High
Quality	High quality	Yes		Moderate quality	Moderate quality	High Quality
Selection	Under a dozen styles to choose from	Yes		Hundreds of designs to choose from	Two styles to choose from	Under a dozen styles to choose from
Fit Reliability	Consistent sizing and fit	Yes		Fit varies per style	Consistent fit	Consistent sizing and fit
Location	Online, Individual National Retailers		Yes	Online, Own Name Brand Stores Nationally	Individual National Retailers	Online, Individual National Retailers
Sales Method	Wholesale & Retail	Yes		Retail Only	Wholesale Only	Wholesale & Retail
Advertising	Social media, direct mail, tradeshow, online marketing		Yes	Television, print ads in magazines	Print ads in magazines, tradeshows	Social media, direct mail, tradeshows

Niche

Porcelynne caters to the public by offering a high quality fit in moderately priced fabrics.

Say how you plan to do your advertising and promotion and what your budget is. Do you plan on sending out press kits? Will you be sending samples out with them and how often will you be sending them? Do you plan on participating in trunk shows, fashion shows, street fairs, or sell online?

Advertising & Promotion

Porcelynne Lingerie has proven each method, with the exception of tradeshows, have worked in obtaining revenue and additional sales accounts. Surprisingly, the most effective (and cheapest) promotion has been blogging, social media marketing and email marketing. After researching and attending several of the intimate apparel tradeshows, Porcelynne Lingerie is well prepared for these shows.

Advertising/Promotion	Description	Frequency	Projected Cost	Revenue Expected
Social Media Advertising	Maintain pages and advertise on Facebook.com, Etsy.com, Shopflick.com and various other methods	Continuous	$50-100 monthly	$1000 month retail
Blogging	Pitch to bloggers on current products and promotions. Upkeep a personal designer blog	Continuous	Free	$500 month retail
Email Marketing	Email marketing campaign with VerticalResponse.com, for notifying customers about business happenings, occasional sales	Monthly	$15-20 monthly	$1000 month retail
Website	Update the website with new merchandise, events, press and awards.	Monthly	$30 monthly	$2000 month wholesale $200 monthly retail
Showroom Sales	Open studios for direct to consumer sales.	Monthly	$15-20 for entertaining	$500 monthly retail
Street Fairs & Sample Sales	Promote brand awareness. Build a customer following. Sell samples, seconds and over cuts	Bi-monthly	$100-200 bi-monthly	$4000 month retail
Press Kits	Samples, press releases and marketing material to targeted media to encourage editorial and feature use	Monthly	$100-200 monthly	$1000 monthly retail $2000 monthly wholesale
Direct Mail Postcard Promotions	Sent to retail buyers. Follow up calls and emails will accompany the postcard and will be conducted by the in-house sales representative	Continuous	$20-50 monthly	$1000 monthly wholesale
Trade Shows	Las Vegas or New York intimates tradeshow *Curve*	Semi-annually	$10,000 annually	$200,000 annually wholesale

Chapter 54
Operations

List the location of your business, the location of your showroom, and the location of your manufacturers.

Operations

Porcelynne Lingerie creates all samples and patterns in house in their design studio. A showroom is located in the front entrance.

Showroom

Porcelynne houses their own showroom to showcase all samples, meet with retailers and provide direct to consumer purchases. The showroom is the entrance area and meeting area. Our showroom is open to the public by appointment during the hours 11am to 6pm Monday through Thursday.

Design Studio

Our design studio is directly behind our showroom and contains a 6x12 foot cutting table for pattern work, an industrial electric cutting machine, 2 industrial overlock machines, 1 industrial coverstitch machine and 2 multi use home machines.

Porcelynne Lingerie
Design Studio & Showroom
261 10th Street, Suite 302
Oakland, CA 94607

Production

Our bamboo collection in produced in a local sewing factory. We work closely with the facility to ensure quality control and see quick turn around times due to our "hands on" approach. Our turnaround times for finished sewn products are 4-6 weeks. Dying takes and additional 1-2 weeks. All payment arrangements for production are COD, with the arrangement that damage merchandise will be refunded for future production cycles.

Our lace design is being manufactured overseas in China. They are creating our lace design exclusively for our use and have signed an exclusivity agreement with us. Turnaround time for this piece is 3 to 4 months.

ABC Sewing**
1234 Mission St.
San Francisco, CA 94103
**Name and address has been changed for this book for proprietary reasons

Outline your manufacturing plans. Where will you manufacture? Will you have a production manager? What do you plan on doing in-house, and what services do you plan to hire out— patterns, samples, cutting, sewing, grading?

Suppliers

Environmentally Friendly Fabrics** based in Los Angeles, CA is our primary supplier for our bamboo fabric blends. All of their fabrics are milled in Los Angeles, so turnaround time for fabric is fairly quickly. Quantities of 300 yards or more receive priority shipping. Payment arrangements have been made on a Net-30 arrangement.

Our elastic trims and other notions are sourced from Fabric World**, also based out of Los Angeles, CA. Turnaround time is immediate. Payment arrangements are COD for these trims.

Clothing Labels**, a Los Angeles based company, provides us with our printed satin name and care labels. In 2009, when we outgrow our needs to meet their minimums, we will be sourcing our printed labels through Awesome Product Design** based in Hong Kong, China.

Porcelynne Lingerie's principal attends the Los Angeles International Textile Tradeshow in February and in October, each year, to obtain additional backup sourcing for our materials.
        **Names have been changed for this book for proprietary reasons

Personnel

Porcelynne Lingerie has a limited staff. The pay schedule is bi-weekly. Porcelynne expects to hire one additional patternmaker in August of 2009 and another in January 2010.

Principal

The owner acts as head designer, elects and purchases fabric & related materials, designs the collection, oversees patterns, works with contractors, invoices and manages the books, and acts as the face behind the name Porcelynne. Owner takes a salary of $50,000 annually. Approximately ¼ of the profits will be paid as additional compensation.

Assistant Patternmaker

The assistant patternmaker works as a skilled freelance contractor. The patternmaker drafts & grades patterns, corrects patterns and sews working samples. Assistant patternmaker pay is $25/hour. Annually, the assistant patternmaker will be paid approximately $7,500, and works approximately 25 hours per month.

If you plan on hiring additional staff, say when. Is it when you reach certain sales goals? How much and how often will you pay your staff?

Sales Representative

A sales representative is expect to join our team for our Fall 2010 collection. They will establishes new accounts and assists in promotional events. The sales rep works as an independent contractor and bills on a commission based on total sales they acquire. Sales reps are paid upon receipt of payment from accounts. Sales reps receive 15% commission of collected sales from which they obtain.

Inventory

Limited quantities of supplies including fabric and notions will be on-site for sample creation purposes. All supplies for production will be delivered directly to the factory for garment construction.

All inventories will initially be stored on-site for thorough quality control. When production quantity exceeds our capacity for storage, we will obtain a quality control storage facility. At this point, we will keep a reasonable amount on-site for direct to consumer sales and emergency re-orders.

Inventory unsold at the end of each selling season will be sold at either discounted wholesale with no requirements for minimum sales or will be sold at discounted retail prices online or at direct-to-consumer events.

Credit Policies

All wholesale orders with new accounts will require a credit card for payment or a COD arrangement. Long standing accounts of one year or longer will be considered for a Net-30 payment arrangement.

If credit has been extended for Net 30 and payment is not received after 90 days, the account will be taken into collections with Trans World Systems or another appropriate collection agency.

Chapter 55
Management and Organization

State here what your business entity is and who is on your team. Include a bio of each person involved and his or her level of involvement in your business. You can include each person's resume as an attached appendix. Include both your staff and independent contractors. Specify who is an employee and who is a contractor. List assistants, interns, bookkeepers, graphic designers, web designers, sales reps, pattern makers, contractors, etc.

Management and Organization

Porcelynne Lingerie is presently operated as a Sole Proprietorship. Day-to-day management is done by the principal owner, Jennifer Lynne Matthews.

Principal

Jennifer Lynne Matthews, also known as Jennifer Lynne in the industry, has been operating Porcelynne Lingerie for over 6 years. Her training is in pattern development and design from the Fashion Institute of Technology in New York City. She has worked in bookkeeping and management for over 15 years for professional businesses: Porcelynne Lingerie, Matthews Benefit Group, Inc. and Faraway Moving Company**.

Ms. Matthews has been a college pattern & draping instructor at the Fashion Institute of Design and Merchandising in San Francisco since 2006. She has also worked as a small business consultant in terms of product development, production contracting and basic business operations. Ms. Matthews is one of the founding owners of the East Bay Fashion Resource, a fashion business consulting firm.

Ms. Matthews is actively involved in the fashion design community in San Francisco and surrounding areas. She is also involved on the Advisory Board for San Francisco's first fashion incubator program, Innovative Fashion Council, is sponsored by the San Francisco Mayor's Office.
    **Name has been changed for this book for proprietary reasons

Professional and Advisory Support

Please see the attached Appendix B* for all advisors and their qualifications.
    *This information has not been provided for this book for proprietary reasons

---

Chapter 56
Financial Plan

List your major milestones for the first year as well as your projected sales for the first year. You also want to list your long term growth projections, your expected expenses and sales over the next five years, and any plans for expansion.

Financial Plan

Production Costs

Below are our estimated production costs for our first collection in 2009. Quantities ordered are based on past sales revenues. This model shows production quantities increase for an allowance for damaged goods at 5% and an additional 25% allowance for reorders and direct sales.

Style Name or Style Number	Total Production Cost	Total Cost of Goods	Total Quantity	Allowance for Direct Sales and Reorders	Allowance for Damaged Goods	Quantity Ordered
Tank Top	$ 24,519.63	$ 7.54	3250	625	125	2500
Tee Shirt	$ 3,133.68	$ 9.61	326	63	13	250
Yoga Pants	$ 4,688.78	$ 12.02	390	75	15	300
Sportsbra	$ 1,416.10	$ 7.23	196	38	8	150
Boyshorts	$ 33,374.25	$ 5.71	5850	1125	225	4500
Brief	$ 11,612.25	$ 5.96	1950	375	75	1500
Total Production Cost	**$ 78,744.68**	**Total Quantity**	11962	2301	461	9200

Direct Fixed Expenses

The direct fixed expenses are directly tied to each collection being produced. These costs will only be incurred when a new collection is designed. Photography costs are minimal due to current and past work relationships.

Collection Photography	Fees
Models	
Photographer	$ 200.00
Hair Stylist	
Make-up Artist	
Photo Stylist	
Photoshop/CD/Images	$ 50.00
Space Rental	
Website	
Total Photography Cost	**$ 250.00**

Tradeshows	Fees
Space Fee	$ 3,750.00
Fixtures/Rentals	$ 250.00
Printed Materials	$ 200.00
Lodging	$ 175.00
Airfare	$ 250.00
Food	$ 200.00
Car Rental	$ 125.00
Total Tradeshow Cost	**$ 4,950.00**

Indirect Fixed Expenses

The indirect fixed expenses are the costs for administrative overhead, marketing and labor. These expenses will occur each month.

Administrative	Monthly Estimate	
Credit Card & Bank Charges	$ 30.00	
Office Supplies	$ 50.00	
Postage & Shipping	$ 25.00	
Telephone	$ 50.00	
Utilities	$ 25.00	
Total Administrative	$ 180.00	
Marketing & Sales		
Advertising	$ 220.00	
Event Fees	$ 115.00	
Printed Material	$ 10.00	
Travel	$ 20.00	
Vehicle Expenses	$ 80.00	
Website	$ 30.00	
Total Marketing & Sales	$ 475.00	
Rent		
Rent	$ 250.00	
Insurance	$ 50.00	
Total Rent	$ 300.00	
	Monthly	Annual Salary
Labor		
Principal	$ 4,166.67	$ 50,000.00
Assistant	$ 625.00	$ 7,500.00
Total Labor	$ 4,791.67	$ 57,500.00

12 Month Profit and Loss Projection

Due to the nature of this industry, sales and revenue are received up to nine months after the initial expenses have occurred.

See the attached Appendix C for 12 month projection.

Five Year Profit and Loss Projection

This profit and loss projection assumes a 10% increase for inflation and 20% growth of the company.

	Total 2009	Total 2010	Total 2011	Total 2012	Total 2013
Income from sales					
Wholesale	$ 211,187.17	$ 357,432.13	$ 49,215.18	$ 617,642.73	$ 49,043.84
Retail	$ 43,301.67	$ 94,282.41	$ 37,601.36	$ 162,920.01	$ 438,105.45
Sales Tax Collected	$ 2,165.08	$ 8,014.01	$ 1,696.12	$ 13,848.20	$ 37,238.96
Gross Revenue	**$ 256,653.92**	**$ 459,728.55**	**$ 98,512.66**	**$ 794,410.94**	**$1,424,388.25**
Variable Cost of Production					
Production Costs	$ 78,744.68	$ 207,885.94	$136,070.80	$ 359,226.91	$ 235,130.34
Total Variable Cost	**$ 78,744.68**	**$ 207,885.94**	**$136,070.80**	**$ 359,226.91**	**$ 35,130.34**
Direct Fixed Cost					
Development Costs	$ 600.00	$ 1,584.00	$ 1,036.80	$ 2,737.15	$ 1,791.59
Photography Costs	$ 550.00	$ 360.00	$ 950.40	$ 622.08	$ 1,642.29
Tradeshow Costs	$ 8,910.00	$ 9,108.00	$ 15,396.48	$ 15,738.62	$ 26,605.12
Sales Tax	$ 2,165.08	$ 8,014.01	$ 11,696.12	$ 13,848.20	$ 37,238.96
Total Direct Fixed Costs	**$ 12,225.08**	**$ 19,066.01**	**$ 29,079.80**	**$ 32,946.06**	**$ 67,277.96**
Income from Production	**$ 165,684.16**	**$ 232,776.60**	**$533,362.07**	**$ 402,237.97**	**$1,121,979.95**
Indirect Fixed Cost					
Administrative	$ 2,160.00	$ 2,376.00	$ 2,613.60	$ 2,874.96	$ 3,162.46
Amortization of Goodwill	$ 43.50	$ 43.50	$ 43.50	$ 43.50	$ 43.50
Depreciation of Equipment	$ 230.00	$ 230.00	$ 230.00	$ 230.00	$ 230.00
Marketing & Sales	$ 5,700.00	$ 6,270.00	$ 6,897.00	$ 7,586.70	$ 8,345.37
Interest on Loan	$ 4,280.43	$ 2,659.39	$ 955.41	$ 0.00	$ 0.00
Administrative Labor	$ 57,500.00	$ 57,500.00	$ 57,500.00	$ 57,500.00	$ 57,500.00
Rent	$ 3,600.00	$ 3,960.00	$ 4,356.00	$ 4,791.60	$ 5,270.76
Total Fixed Costs	**$ 73,513.93**	**$ 73,038.89**	**$ 72,595.51**	**$ 73,026.76**	**$ 74,552.09**
Net Profit	**$ 92,170.22**	**$ 159,737.72**	**$460,766.56**	**$ 329,211.21**	**$1,047,427.86**

5 Year Balance Sheet

Current Assets	Total 2009	Total 2010	Total 2011	Total 2012	Total 2013
Total Cash	$ 260,462.47	$ 499,237.99	$ 1,167,356.77	$1,692,472.77	$ 2,960,219.24
Total Fixed Assets	$ 3,500.00	$ 3,500.00	$ 3,500.00	$ 3,500.00	$ 3,500.00
Total assets	$ 263,962.47	$ 502,737.99	$ 1,170,856.77	$1,695,972.77	$ 2,963,719.24

Liabilities

Note	$ 71,016.55	$ 37,849.06	$ 2,984.65	$ 0.00	$ 0.00
Total Liabilities	$ 71,016.55	$ 37,849.06	$ 2,984.65	$ 0.00	$ 0.00

Capital

Contributed Capital	$ 123,500.00	$ 123,500.00	$ 123,500.00	$ 123,500.00	$ 123,500.00
Net profits	$ 1,153.88	$ 4,730.09	$ 14,155.66	$ 12,515.55	$ 28,607.37
Total Capital	$ 124,653.88	$ 128,230.09	$ 137,655.66	$ 136,015.55	$ 152,107.37

Chapter 57
Appendices

This section includes attachments of any kind that pertain to the business plan. These might include cost sheets for each product, resumes of the owners, a detailed five-year profit and loss projection, copies of orders, and press coverage you've received.

Appendix A: Materials Cost

Style Name or Style Number	Material Costs	Label Cost	Item	Cost Per Yard	Yardage	Total Item Cost	Item	Cost Per Yard	Yardage	Total Item Cost	Item	Cost
Tank Top	$ 3.29	.10	Bamboo	$ 4.15	0.33	$ 1.37	Decorative Elastic	$ 0.25	3.7	$ 0.93		
Tee Shirt	$ 4.11	.10	Bamboo	$ 4.15	0.75	$ 3.11						
Yoga Pants	$ 6.27	.10	Bamboo	$ 4.15	1.15	$ 4.77	2" Elastic	$ 0.50	1	$ 0.50		
Sportsbra	$ 2.73	.10	Bamboo	$ 4.15	0.25	$ 1.04	Decorative Elastic	$ 0.25	0.75	$ 0.19	3/4" Elastic	0.50
Boyshorts	$ 2.71	.10	Bamboo	$ 4.15	0.2	$ 0.83	Decorative Elastic	$ 0.25	3.5	$ 0.88		
Brief	$ 2.71	.10	Bamboo	$ 4.15	0.2	$ 0.83	Decorative Elastic	$ 0.25	3.5	$ 0.88		

Appendix C: 12 Month Financial Projection

	Jan 2009	Feb 2009	Mar 2009	Apr 2009	May 2009	Jun 2009	Jul 2009	Aug 2009	Sep 2009	Oct 2009	Nov 2009	Dec 2009
Income from sales												
Wholesale	$ 2,500.00	$ 2,200.00	$ 2,200.00	$ 2,200.00	$ 2,500.00	$ 2,500.00	$ 2,500.00	$ 62,266.67	$ 62,266.67	$ 62,266.67	$ 3,803.58	$ 3,803.58
Retail	$ 2,000.00	$ 2,000.00	$ 2,000.00	$ 3,200.00	$ 3,200.00	$ 3,200.00	$ 3,200.00	$ 4,900.33	$ 4,900.33	$ 4,900.33	$ 4,900.33	$ 4,900.33
Sales Tax Collected	$ 170.00	$ 170.00	$ 170.00	$ 272.00	$ 272.00	$ 272.00	$ 272.00	$ 416.53	$ 416.53	$ 416.53	$ 416.53	$ 416.53
Gross Revenue	**4,670.00**	**4,370.00**	**4,370.00**	**5,672.00**	**5,972.00**	**5,972.00**	**5,972.00**	**67,583.53**	**67,583.53**	**67,583.53**	**9,210.45**	**9,210.45**
Variable Cost of Production												
Production Costs	$ -	$ -	$ -	$ -	$ -	$ 26,248.23	$ 26,248.23	$ 26,248.23	$ -	$ -	$ -	$ -
Total Variable Cost												
Direct Fixed Cost												
Development Costs	$ -	$ -	$ -	$ -	$ -	$ 200.00	$ 200.00	$ 200.00	$ -	$ -	$ -	$ -
Photography Costs	$ -	$ 250.00	$ -	$ -	$ -	$ -	$ -	$ -	$ 150.00	$ 150.00	$ -	$ -
Tradeshow Costs	$ -	$ -	$ 1,650.00	$ 1,650.00	$ 1,650.00	$ -	$ -	$ -	$ -	$ -	$ 1,080.00	$ 1,080.00
Sales Tax	$ 170.00	$ 170.00	$ 170.00	$ 272.00	$ 272.00	$ 272.00	$ 272.00	$ 416.53	$ 416.53	$ 416.53	$ 416.53	$ 416.53
Total Direct Fixed Costs	**$ -**	**250.00**	**1,650.00**	**1,650.00**	**1,650.00**	**200.00**	**200.00**	**200.00**	**150.00**	**150.00**	**1,080.00**	**1,080.00**
Income from Production	**4,670.00**	**4,120.00**	**2,720.00**	**4,022.00**	**4,322.00**	**5,772.00**	**5,772.00**	**67,383.53**	**67,433.53**	**67,433.53**	**7,230.45**	**7,230.45**
Indirect Fixed Cost												
Administrative	$ 180.00	$ 180.00	$ 180.00	$ 180.00	$ 180.00	$ 180.00	$ 180.00	$ 180.00	$ 180.00	$ 180.00	$ 180.00	$ 180.00
Amortization of Goodwill	$ 3.63	$ 3.63	$ 3.63	$ 3.63	$ 3.63	$ 3.63	$ 3.63	$ 3.63	$ 3.63	$ 3.63	$ 3.63	$ 3.63
Depreciation of Equipment	$ 19.17	$ 19.17	$ 19.17	$ 19.17	$ 19.17	$ 19.17	$ 19.17	$ 19.17	$ 19.17	$ 19.17	$ 19.17	$ 19.17
Marketing & Sales	$ 475.00	$ 475.00	$ 475.00	$ 475.00	$ 475.00	$ 475.00	$ 475.00	$ 475.00	$ 475.00	$ 475.00	$ 475.00	$ 475.00
Interest on Loan	416.67	405.61	395.12	384.28	373.39	362.46	351.48	340.46	329.39	318.27	307.11	295.90
Administrative Labor	$ 4,791.67	$ 4,791.67	$ 4,791.67	$ 4,791.67	$ 4,791.67	$ 4,791.67	$ 4,791.67	$ 4,791.67	$ 4,791.67	$ 4,791.67	$ 4,791.67	$ 4,791.67
Rent	$ 300.00	$ 300.00	$ 300.00	$ 300.00	$ 300.00	$ 300.00	$ 300.00	$ 300.00	$ 300.00	$ 300.00	$ 300.00	$ 300.00
Total Fixed Costs	**6,186.13**	**6,175.37**	**6,164.58**	**6,153.74**	**6,142.85**	**6,131.92**	**6,120.94**	**6,109.92**	**6,098.86**	**6,087.73**	**6,076.57**	**6,065.36**
Net Profit	**(1,516.13)**	**(2,055.37)**	**(3,444.58)**	**(2,131.74)**	**(1,820.85)**	**(359.92)**	**(348.94)**	**$ 61,273.61**	**61,334.68**	**61,345.80**	**$ 1,153.88**	**$ 1,165.08**

Good Luck

I would like to take this opportunity to say good luck in your endeavors with your new business. I hope this book has been of assistance to you in organizing your thoughts and getting your business off the ground or to the next level. I would love to hear from you and how this book has helped out. I will be updating this book regularly and am open to your feedback.

I also plan on writing other books of a similar nature about other areas of this industry, so send me your ideas and requests. You might get a mention in my next book.

You may send your comments by email to comments@eastbayfashionresource.com or you can mail them to our office:

East Bay Fashion Resource
261 10th Street, Suite 302
Oakland, CA 94607

About the Author

Jennifer Lynne Matthews attended Fashion Institute of Technology in New York City and graduated in 1999 with a specialization in intimate apparel. After working in the industry as a stylist and freelance designer, she launched her business, Porcelynne Lingerie in 2002. Jennifer has been consulting with small business startups for 4 years and is presently teaching pattern drafting, draping and sewing at the Fashion Institute of Design and Merchandising in San Francisco.

Jennifer serves on the Advisory Board for the Innovative Fashion Council of San Francisco, the first incubator program in the Bay Area sponsored by the Mayor Office. Jennifer is an active member in the San Francisco Bay Area design community through many outlets, from sponsoring events, education and promotion of new talent.

Prior to opening East Bay Fashion Resource in 2007, Jennifer owned and operated an independent designer co-op in San Francisco's Mission District for 2 years. In early 2008, Jennifer closed the doors to Porcelynne Designer Collective to concentrate on her role as an educator.

East Bay Fashion Resource

The East Bay Fashion Resource (EBFR) is an independent resource structured to educate entrepreneurs on the business of fashion. Offering many services, from product development to business implementation, EBFR has assisted with many start-ups.

Originally founded in 2007, Jennifer Lynne Matthews and accessory designer Misty Rose wanted to provide a centralized resource for the San Francisco bay area design community. EBFR now offers business seminars to give designers, hobbyists or just an individual with an idea, an in depth look at design, finance and the legal aspects of running a fashion design business.

EBFR is now partnering with several other Bay Area firms including the Innovative Fashion Council of San Francisco, Chillin' Productions, Evans Group International and Made In Oakland, a city funded production facility providing jobs and training to our community.